FREE TO BE ME

FREE TO BE ME

REFUGEE STORIES

from the

LESBIAN IMMIGRATION SUPPORT GROUP

Edited by Jane Traies

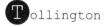

First published in 2021 by Tollington Press, Machynlleth, Wales
www.tollingtonpress.co.uk

A catalogue record for this book is available from the British Library.

ISBN 978-1-909347-19-9

Cover photograph of LISG at Manchester Pride by Jenny White
Back cover photograph by Ruth Fettis

Cover design and typesetting by Helen Sandler

Printed and bound in Wales by Y Lolfa, Talybont, Ceredigion,
on FSC-certified paper

FSC

There was a borehole not far from where my grandmother used to live and that's where I met my second girlfriend... When she helped me lift the water to carry on my head, something just dropped into my heart. —Azanat

I thought, I will be with this lady. And we started being together. Yeah. Like that. —Grace

'Wherever the wind takes us, I am going there tonight!' I just didn't care any more! —Aphrodite-Luna

I thought, 'If I have to live in this country, how will I open up to be me? I will have to change and live another person's life, just to satisfy everybody.' So I decided, maybe I will just go. —Sophie

We had to get out and walk in the bushes all the way to the South African border. We came to a river, the Limpopo. When we saw it, we said, 'Oh my God, this is a big river!' He said, 'We are going to go in and cross that river. Don't walk slowly, because there are crocodiles.' —Chipo

I said, 'What is asylum?' The only understanding I had of an asylum was to do with mental issues, a mental hospital! —Mary

My mum called me and cried on the phone, saying I had brought shame to the family. My father said he never wanted to set his eyes on me again and that the day he does, he will kill me. —Faith

The ways are different here, and at first it was too odd. In the winter, it is so, so cold! But I think I'm better off, far from my own country. Because even if things are so hard, I'm not being beaten, I'm open, I'm free. —Sophie

Lesbian Immigration Support Group members marching at Manchester Pride with the banner that gives this book its title (Photo: Toyin Jimoh)

EDITOR'S NOTE

Free to Be Me is a collection of true stories from refugees and campaigners in the Lesbian Immigration Support Group. Profits from sales of this book will help the group continue to support lesbian and bisexual women seeking asylum in the UK. For many of the contributors – especially those who are still waiting for the Home Office to decide their fate – making their stories public has been an act of courage, a coming-out after many years of hiding.

For women traumatised by homophobic violence, telling their stories sometimes reawakened the horrors of the past; but the tellers were determined not to let that stop them. Their stories include incidents of physical violence, torture, rape and sexual assault, murder, depression and attempted suicide. These accounts can be hard to read, but the women who tell them very much want other people to hear their voices, to walk a little way in their shoes and to acknowledge their truth. Those who do will discover that these are also stories about courage and endurance; about love and community; and above all, about the journey to personal freedom.

CONTENTS

INTRODUCTION

Getting to know the women of the Lesbian Immigration Support Group (LISG) and helping them put together this collection of life stories has been a pleasure and a privilege. It all began in the spring of 2017, when I received an email from a LISG volunteer called Sorrel (whose story is the second in this book). I didn't know Sorrel, but she had heard about my research with older lesbians and my book of lesbian life stories, *Now You See Me*. She wrote to tell me about Grace, a Ugandan woman whose claim for asylum had been rejected because the Home Office did not believe that this African grandmother could possibly be a lesbian. Sorrel explained that LISG were supporting Grace as she prepared a fresh asylum claim, and asked if I might write an expert statement, based on my research, about the difficulties and trauma of coming out as an older lesbian. From the brief facts in the email, I could see that aspects of Grace's story were mirrored in many of the lesbian life stories I had already collected. Of course I would write a statement for her!

Sorrel also told me that Grace was seventy-one. She and I were born in the same year. I sat at my computer, thinking about the differences between my life and hers; I don't think I have ever been more aware of my own privilege than I was on that day. I am an educated white woman living in a country which now has laws to protect LGBTQ+ people; whatever difficulties I faced in my youth because of my sexual orientation, they pale into insignificance beside Grace's struggles. I'm also privileged to be able to engage in research work that gives me immense personal satisfaction. To be told that my work might possibly help someone else felt like an unexpected gift.

I set to work on my letter, but soon realised that I would write far more convincingly if I had actually met the woman I was writing about. So I went to Manchester, the group's base, where I met not only Grace, but Sorrel and another LISG volunteer, Karen S, as well. As it turned out, we had plenty of time to get to know each other in the months that followed, because Grace's fresh claim for asylum was also refused in its turn. She could appeal against that decision, but it would be her very last chance to achieve refugee status and 'leave to remain' in the UK. After that, she would be, in the language of the Home Office, 'appeals rights exhausted' and liable to detention and deportation. In the summer of 2019, we gathered nervously at the tribunal office for Grace's final appeal hearing. Grace was now nearly seventy-four; she had been fighting for asylum in the UK for thirteen years. None of us could bear to think about what would happen if she was rejected this final time.

That was when I first met the other members of LISG. One by one they arrived in the waiting room, bringing life and energy into that gloomy space. Three of us were there to be witnesses in Grace's hearing; all the rest (far more than there were public seats in the courtroom) had come as observers, to offer love and friendship. I had never seen anything quite like this family of sisters. Whatever the outcome of the morning was going to be, Grace was certainly not facing it alone.

As becomes clear in the following pages, her long story did have a happy ending. Grace's barrister was excellent; the judge was unexpectedly sympathetic and (most unusually) he was prepared to tell us there and then that his judgement was going to be positive. The LISG women broke into shouts of laughter and tears of joy. We hugged Grace; we hugged each other; someone even hugged the barrister. Then we wandered off, slightly stunned, to celebrate with tea and toast at the café where I had first met Grace all that time before. Looking round at the group members and volunteers celebrating together like the family they have become, I realised that their story deserved to be better known. That was when the idea of this book was born.

I knew very little, then, about the process of seeking asylum in this country. Working on this book, talking to refugees and asylum seekers and hearing their stories, I have learned fast. The difference between an asylum seeker and a refugee is one of the first lessons for anyone engaging with the system.

A woman fleeing persecution in her own country (or at risk if she returned there) has the right to ask for protection or 'asylum' in another country. This right is enshrined in international and UK law. She is then called an 'asylum seeker' and is entitled to stay while awaiting a decision; if she entered the country illegally, she is no longer 'illegal'. If her application is successful and she is granted asylum, she is called a 'refugee' and may remain in the UK for the time being. Sexual orientation is one reason why someone might seek protection.

There are still many countries which do not tolerate homosexuality. It is easy to forget that until quite recently the UK was one of them. Gay men were in danger of going to prison if caught and, while lesbianism was never illegal here, women could be punished in other ways: physical or sexual violence, rejection by family, losing their jobs or losing custody of children. Such treatment – and worse – is still the fate of lesbians in many countries today. A woman who has fled from such persecution in her home country will already be traumatised and frightened; she will have left behind everything she knew, including home, family and friends; she will very likely have suffered sexual violence and physical abuse as well. If she is claiming asylum on the grounds of her sexual orientation, she will be required to prove to the British authorities that she is, indeed, a lesbian. The authorities are hard to convince: the stories of LGBTQ+ asylum seekers are full of examples of what has been called 'the culture of disbelief'.

How can anyone 'prove' their sexual orientation? LGBTQ+ people are just as diverse as the rest of the population. We differ from each other in all sorts of ways: race, religion, class, socio-economic status and education. We are enormously varied in our appearance and gender presentation. Yet some of the women whose stories appear in this book have been told by Home Office decision-makers that they 'don't look like' lesbians. Such a statement suggests a very narrow, stereotyped set of cultural assumptions about what a lesbian might look like. In fact, the Home Office instructions for recognising a lesbian or gay person, with their emphasis on physical presentation and factual 'evidence' of visits to gay bars and clubs, appears to be based largely on a stereotyped picture of western gay male experience. It is clearly unhelpful in identifying a lesbian or bisexual woman from another cultural background.

Women seeking asylum on the grounds of their sexuality are often rejected because they are judged not to have told a convincing story. It seems that, if a woman's account of her sexual journey does not chime exactly with some predetermined narrative, she will not be believed. She might be judged to have given 'limited responses' to questions about her sexual history, or not to have produced a 'detailed, clear account' of how she 'realised and came to terms with' her sexuality. Her reticence, too, can be interpreted as shiftiness and evasion, though it is entirely understandable in someone who has been hiding her sexuality for fear of the consequences of speaking out, and who might still be burdened by fear and shame. Even in an apparently safe environment, it may not be possible for such a person to express her feelings or experiences articulately; as the stories in this book show, the Home Office rarely feels like a safe environment.

So, every step along the way to refugee status depends on someone in authority believing your story. But when it comes to being believed – or simply being taken seriously – women, people of colour and members of the LGBTQ+ community always start at a disadvantage. If you happen to own all three of those identities, as do most of the contributors to this book, your fight is going to be very hard indeed. In recent years, the struggles of people seeking asylum on the grounds of their sexual orientation have become better known in the LGBTQ+ community. We have learned that the Home Office is more likely to listen to someone with allies and advocates who are prepared to use their own experience – and their privilege – to argue on that person's behalf. Groups have grown up in many major cities in the UK to provide voluntary support. (See the list at the back of this book.) LISG is different from the others, in that it provides specifically for the needs of lesbian and bisexual women.

Free to Be Me is a selection of life stories told by thirteen women who have been part of LISG at various times, whether as group members from around the world who have claimed asylum in the UK, and/or as volunteers, most of whom grew up here. Through their varied experiences, they also tell the story of LISG itself: how it began and what it does.

Putting the book together has been a collaborative effort. All but one of the stories began as recorded conversations (the coronavirus 'lockdown' came towards the end of that process and meant that one woman, Sorrel, wrote her story herself). The interviews were then transcribed to form texts which we could work on together, editing and polishing the transcripts until we were happy with them. The contributors include women from a range of different countries and cultural back-grounds; some appear here under their real names and some have chosen pseudonyms. The youngest is in her late twenties and the oldest is Grace, now in her mid seventies. Hers is the first story.

Jane Traies, Sussex, January 2021

GRACE

As described in the Introduction, Grace was seventy-one when we first met. Her age made her unusual among people seeking asylum; the other contributors to this book are much younger. Grace fled to the UK in 2006, but it was 2013 before she was able to register her asylum claim and it was not granted until 2019. Although I had known her for some time by then, and had been with her on the day of her final appeal hearing, I had never heard her story in full until we recorded it for this collection. Grace's first language is Luganda, and she speaks English less fluently than many of the other contributors. Nevertheless, she describes very vividly a long and eventful life that began in pre-independence Uganda just after the Second World War.

Grace was born in 1945, in Kikwanda, a village in what was then the sub-country of Uganda called Busiro. She was brought up by a kind and loving aunt, to take pressure off her parents. When another little cousin the same age was also taken in by her aunt, the two became like brother and sister. As she told me about her childhood, I thought I could see, in the determined and naughty little five-year-old Grace, a reflection of the strength of character that has sustained her through so many terrible challenges since then.

When we were five, they decided to send us to the nearest school. We went there on foot. A long way! The boys had their own school room, and the girls had theirs, but they were very close together. And I remember that whenever I heard my brother crying – because I knew his voice – sometimes I didn't even ask my teacher, I just went out to see why he was crying. I just got up and left.

I would ask him, 'Why are you crying?' And he would say, 'That one has beat me.' And I would slap that boy who hit him, and then run back to my class.

But one day, the boys' teacher followed me. When I entered my class, he said to my teacher, 'That girl has been in our class, and has been hitting somebody.'

And my teacher asked me, 'Grace, what have you been doing there?'

I said, 'Nothing!' I was very angry.

And she said, 'Are you sure? I shall have to smack you.'

So I said, 'I heard my cousin crying, and I left to go and see why he was crying. When he told me who was the one that was hitting him, I just wanted to lift my hand, straight away!'

They started laughing, and my teacher said, 'If you do it again, I'm going to smack you and send you back to your home, you understand? Don't beat him again!'

And I said, 'Okay, I not do it again,' and stayed in my class.

Our parents would sometimes put food in our pockets at night, to take to school in the morning. When I had some, I would just leave my class to go and find where my brother was, and start eating with him.

The teachers said, 'Why don't you wait here for us to give you your food?'

'This is my food. I like to eat it with my brother.'

And I gave them so much trouble that in the end they said, 'You go back home, and come next year.' They told my aunt, 'We think this one is too young. We don't like to smack her every time. We talk to her, but she doesn't understand!' And they asked her if I could come the next year, when I had grown up.

'Pen pals'

Grace did return the next year and started learning. Her family moved her to a distant boarding school while she was still small, visiting her every two weeks; there were tears each time they parted. Then in secondary school she got into a different kind of trouble with the staff.

Because we were Catholics, we were not supposed to do certain things. We had to have very good behaviour. Not like here, with boyfriends. No boyfriends! The nuns didn't like them. Good behaviour!

But I remember that when I was in secondary school, we

used to have some white ladies coming to teach us music, and they started to talk about 'pen pals'. They used to write letters to their white girl friends – pen pals – in this country. They were writing their letters, saying 'My name is So-and-so and I am at this school, and I like you very much...' Things like that. And they started to give us those pen pals. I had one. She was in the UK. At that time, I didn't know English, and an older girl, my friend, who was in a higher class, helped me with what to write.

But when the nuns found me writing this, they said to me, 'We don't like you doing this! Who has given you this address?'

I said, 'Mrs Smith – she gives us pen pals.'

They were *very* annoyed. 'We don't want you to do this! Why do you do like this?'

And when the term ended, they told my parents, 'Take her to another school! We don't like this kind of girl.'

So that was why I left. Now, when I think about it, and remember this lady, I do wonder... She used to come with a guitar and some books, to teach us to sing, and she would say, 'I have my pen pal, my friend...' But then, we didn't know the meaning of it. Because maybe it was... When I came here, to the UK, I saw women like that. And then I thought, this might have been about lesbians. Maybe. Pen pals. But at that time, I didn't know anything about it.

After that I went to a commercial school, to learn typing, and I qualified as a copy typist. I was seventeen or eighteen by then. I started work in a government office, because my dad was also working there and he had friends there.

Two unhappy matches

Then one of my aunts – not the one that brought me up, but another of my dad's sisters – said, 'Now you are old enough, you have to marry.' My dad would have preferred me not to marry at that time. He wanted me to continue working. But that aunt said, 'No, don't spoil the girl, she has to marry.'

They found me a man, who I married. He wasn't my religion. He was a Muslim – that's why my dad didn't like him – but I think they liked his money or something, I don't know. I didn't know he was a Muslim. He was called Moses. It's an African man's name. Catholics can use it. Protestants can use it. They used that name because they didn't like to say 'Mohammed'. He knew that I was Catholic, and Catholics do not like Muslims, that's why he got another name.

I didn't like that man, but they forced me to marry him. We weren't married in church; it was an African marriage. He forced me to do some things… He treated me in a bad way. What could I do? With that man I got my firstborn. It was a girl. But after I'd been with him only two years, I disappeared from him. I went to another district, to a friend of my aunt, and I stayed there. He understood I was a Catholic, but he had also got another woman. He had two wives, at the time when I was with him. So I just disappeared.

My aunt was very disappointed, but my dad understood. I went away and kept quiet; but he was worried that someone would find out where I was. It took about three years for them to find me. So I came back home. I came with my child, and gave her to my mum, to live with her. I couldn't go to work in another district, with her. So my daughter stayed with my mum, but when I got money I sent it to her and my dad. And they told me, as you have already got a child, and you have to support it, you have to get another man.

So I went away to another district to work, and I got another man.

I only wanted to get a man to get children. But, as you know, the real African way is that to have children you have to be married. You can't get a baby here, and then another from here, and another from there – you must marry the man. I already knew I didn't really want a man in my life. I didn't like to be with a man. I didn't feel like a girl. In my heart, I was not a girl – I wanted to be a man. I was feeling like a man. I saw the men – they have the power. They do this and that...

So I was with this man, and I got children from him. Four of them, in a difficult life. When I had the first two, things were not so bad, but with the other two, life was difficult. He got another woman, and they did *wicca* things to me. You understand when I say *wicca* things? There are some witch doctors; and they sent me some things which stabbed me, some bad devil's things, which affected me and made me feel bad. And that man beat me very badly. Some of the villagers came, because we were making such a noise.

I said, 'I have to go!' I packed some of my things, and asked him to give me my kids – and he refused. I didn't like to leave my kids with him, because I knew his other wife was going to treat them very badly. But when he refused, I had to go, all alone: I collected all my things and packed them on the cart, and I disappeared.

An independent woman

So now Grace had 'disappeared' from two partners. She was still working, and when she heard that some of her children were indeed being mistreated, she managed to take two of them to live with her. Meanwhile, she helped her parents to keep her first daughter in school. All of this was a struggle, until the children were a little older.

Then I decided to buy a small plot and build myself a house. It was a nice bit of a house, and we could stay together there. And then that man wanted to come back to me! I refused. He had already married another woman, so I said, 'You can't come here. And you have to give me my children!' At that time, he was not well. That's why he wanted to be with me, because I was working. Huh.

Then I left the government job and I joined Action Aid. A classmate of mine who was working there said, 'Grace, come and join me.' This lady, who was older than me, said,

'You have suffered a lot. We have this organisation – come and join with us!' I went there first as a cleaner. The salary was not bad, and I was suffering where I was, so I was happy that I joined. I got money, I started getting involved with some white people, and I felt I was doing something. Action Aid had just started in our country and we were very small, not many in the office, only about ten people. So, I worked there for about six or seven years. They taught me how to drive a motor cycle. And I was happy at that time. I was alone, and happy to be with my children, sending them to nice schools.

Family tragedies

My eldest girl, who was now sixteen, went to teacher training school. She finished her training, but she had only been working about one year when she got HIV. She died when she was nineteen years old. Eh! And she left a child, a boy of three years old. Then his dad, my son-in-law, also died. My daughter died in 1992, and her man died in '95. I took the kid to stay with me. He lived with me and I sent him to school...

This boy also had HIV. When he was five, he began to be sick all the time, but I was scared to take him to the hospital. Then some of my friends said to me, 'Grace, be brave. You lost your child – but did you die when your daughter died?'

I said, 'No.'

And they said, 'Be brave, take the kid to hospital. If they say he's okay, you will be glad, and if they say he's sick, he'll get medicine.'

So, I took him to the Lady May hospital. And they found that he was HIV. Oh. That hit me hard. But they counselled me, and they said I must try to bring him every time, to get medicine.

At that same time, my contract at Action Aid finished and they didn't renew it. Those white people say that they wanted to give power to African people, so they set up the organisation and then they came back to the UK. But when Africans took over, they started to look out for their own people. And my contract, they didn't renew it. I was happy with those white people; but when they decided to give up – well, that's why I lost my job. So, at that time I started to become very sad. I stayed in my home. I had no work. But I continued taking the boy to the hospital.

When he was thirteen – he was in Primary 7 – the doctor told me, 'You must be brave and tell that boy you are not his mum, you are his grandma. Because when he grows up and you say, "I didn't tell you," he will say, "Why?" and we may have a problem.'

I said that I wouldn't want him to know about his mum, because it would make me sad. But one day, I asked God, 'Help me to do this thing.' I woke up in the morning, I went and cut bits in my garden, I finished and cleaned myself up, and then I called him: 'Bernard, come here!'

And he came, and I said, 'Bernard, I want to tell you something. Something that you didn't know. I don't know what you are going to think – it is not good – but I'd like you to know it while I'm still alive.'

And he said, 'Mum, what do you want to tell me? No!' because he was afraid. He saw my eyes and he said, 'Mum, are you starting to cry?'

And I said, 'No, I'm not crying, but I feel pain.'

And he said, 'Are you sick?'

'No. But what I am telling you, while I am still alive, is – me, I am your grandma. I am no longer your mum. I didn't want to tell you when you were still young, because I knew it was going to hurt you, as it hurts me. You are my grandson. My daughter – your mum – died.'

And I showed him her picture. When she was still young, when she was a young mother.

And he gasped. He said, 'I didn't know. I thought my mum had gone abroad. To London or America. Some of the

23

people who have gone there didn't come back. That was why I thought it. But I wasn't sure.' And then he said, 'I heard some rumours.'

I asked him, 'Who told you?'

'I'm not going to tell you. But I was not sure about it.'

I started crying, and when he saw me cry, he started crying.

I said, 'No. Bernard. Stop crying. When you start crying you hurt me very much. I am happy, even though my daughter died, that you are also my son. I call you my son. You are brave, and I am also going to be brave.'

And he said, 'Okay.'

And I said, 'God will help us.'

You see? But I saw him, sometimes, looking at me...

He's still in Uganda. I don't know how I could bring him here. But we are still in touch, yes. Very much. He's finished university! And he is still alive. Last time we spoke, he told me, 'Mummy, I went to the hospital, but sometimes they don't have medicine. They give me some, but last time I didn't get a certain one...'

I was feeling very sad. But at the same time, he told me, 'Mummy, I'm happy. I have a wife and a child.' (Last year he had told me, 'Yeah! I'm expecting a kid!') The baby has *not* got HIV and he told me his wife has not got HIV. When he told me that, I took two hours talking with him. The next day, I bought a card with ten pounds on it, to talk to him. Phew. They are happy. And I'm happy, because I spent a long time struggling with that boy, taking him to hospital. And I was not expecting him to live this long. That's why I thank God!

'I will be with this lady'

While Grace was still living in Uganda, she joined a group of women who got together to learn to keep livestock. She made a special connection with one of them. Judith was from another tribe and had moved to the village with a group of friends. She and Grace had both been married and had encountered similar problems.

So I met Judith, and we started talking with each other, and she was telling me her story. I took a time, listening to her. And, after a time, I started to go and visit her, and she started to come and visit me, because we were both planning how to breed pigs, and so on. She wanted us to work together at my house.

She said, 'Grace, I have just a little place. What if we get two pigs each and keep them in the same yard, here? You have space.'

I said to Judith, 'You have friends from your own country, why don't you put the pigs there?'

She said, 'They are married. They can't make time for me. I don't mind, but as you are alone, and I am alone, we can work together.'

And we did.

When the time came to kill the pigs, we were waiting, and we sat down and talked to each other. She told me about the problems with her marriage, and me, I told her the same. Hm...

Until I thought, I will be with this lady. And we started being together. Yeah. Like that.

I was very happy, because we understood each other. And also, I was happy that she wasn't from my place, but from somewhere else, because she wasn't going to go and tell my neighbours this and that – no.

Her friends didn't know. She said to me, 'I don't think people should know about me and you. I told them, this is my friend.' She used to come to my house. My children called her Auntie – they didn't know. Even my sisters didn't know about it. We kept it very quiet.

But the problem was that some people from her district came and visited her friends. And they found out that she was at my house. Her friends said, 'She goes to visit a lady... and they do this and that...'

And they said, 'Hmmm...'

Dangerous rumours

Then some people said to me, 'Grace, we heard these rumours about you, this and this and this…'

And I said, 'No!' I said, 'They are a liar. We are just tending pigs here.'

Because there was no way I could tell them.

But some people started talking. Then boys from where Judith lived kept coming to my house. And they started spreading rumours about us, saying that we did certain things, and that we had sex with each other, and so on.

And at first, I just said, 'It isn't true, send those boys away and take no notice of them!'

Even so, people began to listen to them, and they asked me if what they said was true.

I said, 'No, just ignore them – calm down.'

And I kept quiet. But some of my friends, they said, 'Grace, what about this and this?'

Other friends said, 'No, Grace would not do like that. She is working in the church, and so forth. She couldn't do like that.'

But some said, 'What is going on? That woman has her own house – why is she always coming to stay here?'

And I told them, 'She has to stay here because she has to clean out her pigs.' Because by that time we had started to have many little pigs. I used to go to her place, but I didn't stay there, because I had my kids at my place; and because if people were to say, 'Oh Grace is always sleeping here,' they might have understood.

Some of my friends said, 'Hm, Grace might be like that. We must find out the truth.'

People were following us about all the time, following us about – which I didn't know, until Mary, a friend in the group, told me, 'Grace, they have started to do this and that… Be careful!' And when I saw what was going on, I was frightened.

So, when I had a chance to get away, I took it. The people from the UK who taught us about the poultry and the pigs gave us a conference where we met all the other groups. And one of the people there was the friend who took me to Action Aid. I talked to her, and she said that she could arrange for me to go to a different country, through one of the organisations like Action Aid or Oxfam. You needed an invitation from someone in that country who would sponsor you, and she arranged that for me. That was how I came here.

I talked to Judith. I told her, 'Let me see if I get a chance. Let me go first, and if I can get a chance, I can call you, and you can follow me later.'

She said, 'Okay.'

And I told her, 'Be careful!'

So after that she started not to come to my place, and she sold her pigs.

And when I had that chance to come here, to the UK, I stayed. I had a visitor's visa, but I stayed on. That was in 2006. I thought that if there was a chance, Judith could come too.

Out of the frying pan...

Grace found herself in a vulnerable situation, in a new country where she was unable to work legally. Unfortunately there were people around who were all too willing to exploit this.

When I came here, what I didn't know was, that lesbians are allowed here. No one was telling me that. I was scared that if these white people knew that about me, they might send me back. That's why I didn't say anything.

After two weeks, the friend I had been staying with said, 'I'm going to send you to a friend of mine to stay for a few weeks, and after that we can see what we are going to do next.' And her friends came and collected me and took me to their place. When these people first saw me, they asked me, 'Where is your passport? Someone might take it from you. Give it to us! We are working everything out for you with the Home Office.' So I gave them my passport, and I was expecting them to do something for me.

I started working there, but she was not treating me well – quite the opposite. She wasn't one of our tribe; they were Nigerians, so I didn't know their language, and when they were speaking English, sometimes I didn't understand it properly. I thought they were going to help me, but they didn't. I was working hard, and looking after the two kids aged four and two, just to get food. They didn't pay me. They never let me go out. One day, when I was feeling not well, they took me to the hospital, but when I was finished, I had to call them and they came and collected me. I had no way of going anywhere on my own. On Sundays I couldn't even go to the church I went to when I first arrived, because they said to me, 'When people see you, they will take you back to your country.' They frightened me. I was trapped.

Until one day, a lady came and visited them, when they were not there. She found me there, and she saw how they were treating me. She was a born-again Christian. She asked me some questions. She said, 'Don't tell them anything about this. But I know how they treat you and I will do something.'

After about a year, she said to me, 'One day you must go to a certain place and we will come and take you away somewhere.'

I didn't tell her that they had taken my passport. I kept quiet for about a week, and then I asked the lady I lived with, 'I'd like to have my passport.'

And she shouted – she had a big voice – 'Why do you want your passport? You can't have it. We have filled in the forms and sent it off to the Home Office for you, and they have not yet returned it. Why do you want it? Have you been talking to somebody?'

'No, nobody. I'm not going anywhere.'

I kept quiet after that. And I started to be worried about my passport. One day, I asked them if I could go to the market to buy something, but the lady said, 'No. I will take you.' I was a prisoner.

But when she was sleeping, I got out some of my things, and I took my bag; I left some of my clothes behind, but I got out. I went to the church where that born-again lady was a pastor. And I told her everything. I told her about my passport. And she said, 'Okay, don't worry. I'm going to take you to the Home Office.'

Judith

Grace went to stay with a friend of the woman who had helped her, where she did a little work for them, ate well and was given money for clothes, before being passed on to a London household under a similar arrangement. They told Grace how to send money home to her children, but still no one lodged her asylum claim. Meanwhile, Judith's situation was very much on Grace's mind and she did the only thing she could to help.

I sent money to Judith, but separately because I didn't want my children to know. What I sent her was a lot – about ten thousand shillings in our money.

But there was a time when she told me, 'Grace, I am going back to my home country. Because people have started asking me questions about why I came here, and rumours are circulating. I'm going back.'

But she went to another part because, where she had lived before, they had already heard that she was 'like that'. And they knew that her friend was Muganda – that was me – we were of different tribes.

She had children but they were grown up. And now they were trying to find out where I lived, to find my house. She said, 'Can you try and get me to where you are?'

But I told her, 'My dear, when you first come here it is very difficult. You stay there.' She had said she wanted to go to my place and see how the kids were and so on, but I told her, 'Don't go to my place, don't go there. My children have no problem with you, but other people may have a problem.'

And she said, 'Okay.'

But she did go to my house, bringing food and other things, and people saw her. She stayed there two days, and people knew she was there, and they came to the house. When she saw the people she was scared, and went back to one of her friends near her home, and stayed there. But I think some people had recognised her. And they caught her. And they killed her.

Not only had Judith been murdered, but when her body was found, no one would come forward to help the police. Grace's children were questioned but there was little they could tell the officers. Eventually, Judith's family were allowed to take her body. Grace was the last to hear the terrible news – from the friend who had warned her to be careful.

After three weeks, Mary called me and told me, 'Grace, your friend has been murdered.' I was very sad. I said to myself, 'I told her not to come there! Why did she go to my place?'

Later, when I was giving my evidence to the Home Office, they said, 'This story cannot be true; if she had been murdered, the police would have taken action.' But what could they do? There was no evidence.

I heard that some villagers came at night and killed my pigs. They burned down the place where we kept the pigs, and stole things, they knocked my house about, and my children ran away. They didn't know where one of my boys went, because he was meant to report to the police, but I think he gave the police some money to let him go, and after that they don't know where he went. I heard a rumour that he was with some neighbours, but I'm scared because I don't know if he's still alive. I have sent some money to some people, to check and see where he is, but they took the money and haven't done anything. I was very scared, and I asked God to help me.

I keep in touch with my daughter. She hasn't gone back to my house, but one of my sisters told me that some people had come on to my plot and destroyed my house. They built a small house on my plot and are living there. No one has stopped them.

No visa, no passport, no home

Grace was also facing difficulties in England. She had come to the UK on a visitor's visa, and had to rely on other people to help her obtain permission to stay. In addition, she was developing health problems.

When I first went to London, the man I was staying with filled in forms for me. He didn't explain all the forms, he just said, 'Sign here,' and I didn't read them all. He said, 'In a month or two you will get a reply.'

I was happy, I thought that he was a good man who would not do bad things. He said he was known in the Home Office and had friends working there. Also, he took money from me that he said he would pay to the Home Office people. After three months the reply came, and my claim was refused. I only understood later that those forms were just asking them to renew my visa – not an asylum claim. And he did not pay them, and he did not give me back my money. And I was very sad.

That was why I moved to live with some other people. But this was the time when I started having asthma.

Grace was still registered with a GP in Oldham, and could not access medical help or prescriptions in London without her passport, which of course she didn't have. So she returned to the northwest to be near her doctor. There, her immigration status became more pressing.

So I came back. Remember that born-again pastor who helped me? I went back to her. By this time the Home Office had started writing me letters, they wanted me to see an adviser and all this, and I took all these papers to her. She wanted to take me to the Home Office; but other people were telling me, 'If you go there, they will send you back.' I didn't know what to do.

One day, I met a gentleman on a bus. He spoke to me in my own language: 'Hello young lady, how are you?' He was Ugandan, and he asked me where I was from and what I was doing, and we chatted. He said, 'Do you know a lady called Gladys?'

I said, 'Yes! She is my friend!'

'Tell her I will come and see her.'

And when I told her, she said, 'Grace, you are lucky! He can give us advice about the Home Office.' She phoned him and he came next day.

He advised me, and he asked me about everything. He said, 'You are a lesbian? Oh, when you were first at the airport you should have said that! These people here don't mind about it.'

And I said, 'Is that true?

He said, 'We will go to the Home Office next week.'

But I was scared, because I was not sure about him. But Gladys said it would be okay. He called the Home Office and he made an appointment. He was a good man. And the Home office phoned me and asked me everything. Sometimes they didn't understand my pronouncing of words, but they filled in a form and they promised to call me.

Good Samaritans

And then that pastor who was helping me, moved away. She sold her house and went somewhere else; I had no contact with her at all. So, I lost her. And after that pastor left, I had nowhere to stay. I couldn't stay with my friend Gladys, in case they took away her benefits. So, I would go to the born-again church, and sometimes I would sleep there overnight.

One day – it was winter – I was in the church, and a young lady who was a nurse saw me. She said, 'My aunt, what's wrong with you?'

And they said, 'Oh this lady has asthma.'

She helped me. She said, 'Oh my dear! Where are you staying?'

I said, 'Nowhere.'

And she said, 'Okay. Let me take you to my place. Don't be scared of me, I am a nurse and I will help you.'

And I told her all about the Home Office, and what that man did, and she said, 'Okay, I will tell you what to do.'

She used to work nights, and one day I took a call and it was the Home Office. They told me they were going to give me an appointment. My friend couldn't go with me because she was working, but she helped me prepare for the questions they might ask. Gladys was afraid to go with me in case they asked her awkward questions, so I had to go alone. I woke up early, and went to the station. Since I had been working in London, I was not afraid to go up and down on a train.

So, I got to the Home Office. They asked me many questions, but I was coughing so much I couldn't answer.

They said, 'Could you come back when you are better?'

And I said, 'No, I have suffered a long time.'

When they discovered how far away I was living, they said, 'Wouldn't you like to stay here with us tonight, and talk again tomorrow?'

But I said no, because I was scared that if I stayed there, they would send me back to Uganda! So, they asked me lots of questions and then I went back. And that was how I started with the Home Office, in 2013.

They gave me a solicitor, and when I was talking to her, she asked me where I came from, and why. She knew a lady called Prossy, who also comes from Uganda, and she said, 'I will put you in touch, perhaps she can help you.'

So I went to meet Prossy, and we talked together, and that's how I found LISG. Prossy is a good lady, and has helped so many people.

But the Home Office refused me. They said I was lying, and I said, 'What am I going to do?'

I had told them everything, all the stories I told them, and they asked me this and that, but they didn't believe me.

Why do they like to believe we tell lies? If it really was safe for me to go back, I wouldn't have wanted to stay here! Because when I came here, I had no high blood pressure, I had no asthma. Now, I spend all my years suffering like that!

But I am safe now, so I'm happy about that. After I was refused, I had to get another solicitor – and that one was very good. And the barrister, he was a good guy. So, after thirteen years in the UK, and six years fighting with the Home Office, I got my stay. I was lucky that day!

~

Grace has found a special place in the LISG family. The younger members call her 'Mama Grace' and treat her with loving respect. She was also, indirectly, the reason that the next contributor, Sorrel, joined the group.

SORREL

Both Grace and Sorrel have passed their seventieth birthdays, so could easily have found a place in my collection of older lesbian life stories, Now You See Me. Although they come from different countries – Grace from Uganda and Sorrel from the UK – they have some experiences in common. For instance, each was a wife and mother before having her first lesbian relationship. Each felt the need to conceal that relationship: Sorrel talks here about the days when women like her could lose their jobs and custody of their children, just because of their sexuality. In the 1980s, she and her partner had to be careful 'never to hug in front of a window, in case a neighbour saw us'.

Sorrel now lives in the Calder Valley in the north of England, where the towns of Todmorden and Hebden Bridge have strong, well-established lesbian communities. She was a founder member of the Valley Sisters, a fundraising group supporting women's causes. When they organised an event to raise money for LISG, Sorrel was introduced to Grace. It is a touching story: overwhelmed by what Grace had been through, she decided to volunteer with LISG, and has been with the group ever since.

My mum's family came from Ayrshire in Scotland and my dad's family from London and Cornwall. My parents met in West Africa, near Accra, in 1945; my mother was a nurse and my father was in the Army. They moved back to the UK in 1948 and I was born in Scotland in 1950. So I was born into army life. It was tough for my mother, who had ill health and was always packing and unpacking as we constantly moved, and tough for my sister and me. When I was three, we moved to Germany and moved three times in that country. By the age of eleven, I had been to six schools. I was nearly six when we moved to Hong Kong, where we stayed for two and a half years. We lived out in the New Territories on mainland China and then on Hong Kong island. I learnt to swim in lovely warm sea; I still feel I am a sea creature.

I began to understand – but did not have the language to express my thoughts – that the British families were living in someone else's country. We had a live-in help, which all army families had. I loved Ah Chi. When I found out she had a daughter my age, I asked why she didn't live with her. She explained she needed the money to pay for her daughter's education. That made me think. I knew I went to an army school, where there were no Chinese students, and I didn't think my parents paid for my education. Later I understood about colonisation.

'Outwardly fitting in'

We moved back to England in 1959 and lived in Sheffield. I loved sport and was a tomboy, happiest when climbing trees, making dens, riding my bike. My mother despaired. At thirteen I was sent to boarding school. It was a day school, but took in thirty boarders. I made lasting friendships there. I remember in my first month another girl asked me to get into bed with her. I didn't really like her, but I did. She started touching me and I didn't like that, so quickly went back to my own bed. I never really thought about my sexuality. I had never heard of the word lesbian. I had learnt to fit in and I was a star at outwardly fitting in!

Every now and again we would go on blind dates with boys. In this way I met the boy I later married. I could always talk to him; looking back we were like best mates rather than lovers. I think I fell in love with him because when he went to kiss me, he seemed to know it wasn't what I wanted and he backed off.

At eighteen I got a place at Chelsea College of Physical Education, embarking on a three-year teacher training course. Again, I was in an all-women environment. Later, I realised that most of the staff were lesbian and I knew I felt very comfortable around women, but nothing happened. I had one proposition. One day, during a summer heatwave, I was lying on the beach when a woman approached me and asked if I would like to see her etchings! I was curious, but not curious enough.

I married in 1971 and taught PE in an all-girls comprehensive school in Bradford. I loved teaching contemporary dance and formed a lunchtime dance club. They were a wonderful group and they showcased their work at different school events. Dance was also a way in to movement and exercise, particularly with older girls who hated PE. I encouraged girls to bring in their music and they began to create their own dances. Sadly, some staff were not happy and felt that girls bringing music to school was not acceptable So that stopped, even though I argued for all the benefits.

I had my first daughter in 1975 and by 1979 I had three small children. It was after my third child was born that I met Di. This meeting was to be a life-changing moment for me. Di was also married and had two small children. We immediately clicked; we started going to yoga together and then talking and talking. Di told me about her feelings for women. I was very supportive and encouraged her to contact Lesbian Line. I still did not face my own sexuality. I was busy reading anything feminist I could find. I read magazines like *Spare Rib* and *Trouble and Strife* and books by Simone de Beauvoir, Marge Piercy, Adrienne Rich, Audre Lorde, Mary Daly, Andrea Dworkin… It was an explosion of consciousness raising.

Awakening

Then two things happened. Di told me she was going away for a weekend with a friend. I felt jealous; I knew that I wanted to go away with Di. The second thing was that I was watching a TV programme about a women's centre where the majority of the workers and volunteers were lesbian. I looked at the women and I could see myself: I was beginning to make connections with myself. After this awakening, Di and I became lovers. It was totally liberating. I was alive! The world had changed! At last I understood.

It took me nearly three years from meeting Di to move out of my marriage. It felt as if I kept edging towards the cliff edge but couldn't jump. I couldn't take the leap into the unknown. I had three children. Their father was kind and committed to being a good father; what was I doing? I tried finishing with Di, but that didn't work. It just made me realise that this is who I am. I was making everyone miserable. I wanted to be out, not closeted. I knew who I was – a lesbian and a feminist – and I couldn't carry on pretending. I told the children that I was a lesbian and that their father and I were going to live separately. I was supported in this by their father. We did our best to ensure they knew it was not their fault and we both still loved them completely. The children lived with me but saw him and his family very regularly. Looking back, we were very fortunate. I knew women who lost custody of their children just because they were lesbian.

Di and I found places to live that were opposite one another, just a quiet back street separating us. We had hoped we could live together, but with five children in one house we felt that our relationship would get completely lost and we agreed to live separately.

I embarked on a degree in women's studies at Bradford University. I became more and more political, more and more radical in my feminist thinking. I studied part time and mainly worked on essays and reading in the evening. I had joined the Rape Crisis collective but the phone line was only open in the evening and now that I lived on my own with the children it became more difficult for me to continue. Di and I had set up a support group for women, liaising with local health visitors. We set up a keep fit and social group which was very successful. We did this voluntarily, but after a year two community workers came to a class and I was offered work in running keep fit classes on two housing estates in Bradford. Before that, Di and I didn't know any other out lesbians or feminists.

Dream job

I desperately needed a job. Eventually I successfully applied for a job at Bradford College. I became an organiser in adult education. It was a dream job for me, I absolutely loved it. I was full of ideas. It was 1986. I had a lot of freedom in this job which was to organise a programme of evening adult education classes, using the facilities of the entire college. The first women's classes I organised were assertiveness for women and car maintenance for women. I remember being told that the courses could only run if there were sufficient students. As it happened, so many women enrolled for the car maintenance we were able to run two classes. Over the years we had classes for women in plumbing, electrics, plastering, woodwork, brickwork. It was such an exciting time. It felt for a moment we were opening up the world in ways our fore-sisters never could have imagined. Many hundreds of women took these opportunities and learned manual skills for the first time.

I was aware that I had built up respect in the department for equal opportunities and inclusivity. I started to organise British Sign Language (BSL) courses for beginners, later progressing to Levels 1, 2, and 3. We made a significant appointment, a Deaf woman, Mary, whose work was to oversee and develop the BSL provision. She and I worked tirelessly to encourage Deaf people to teach the sign language classes. With tenacity, we organised a BTEC teaching qualification completely taught in BSL. The department went on to employ nine part-time Deaf tutors.

Sadly, we lost all this provision, for several reasons. Women's rights were being attacked. A man in Carlisle brought a sex discrimination case against his local college, arguing that it was against the law to run self-defence for women when there was no self-defence for men. He won! This decision had a huge impact nationally. I was virtually told I couldn't continue to run women-only courses. This was around 1995. Another reason for the demise of adult education was that non-vocational education courses (those that did not directly lead to a qualification) were also being attacked and funding was cut year by year. We struggled on; at least the sign language courses were vocational, they would be safe. I left the college in 1998, as did my colleague Mary. After we left, no one continued to organise this provision. That was a loss.

Changes

In 1988, Clause 28 had become a reality; this was a law to prohibit the promotion of homosexuality by local authorities. This directly affected schools and libraries and it was no longer possible to give positive images of lesbians and gay men. Children living with gay or lesbian parents were seen as 'pretend' families; they were not real. Clause 28 did not get repealed in the UK until November 2003. Di and I were always anxious that we might get reported to Social Services. We were aware never to hug in front of a window in case a neighbour saw us.

We continued to live on opposite sides of the road but, when the children began to leave, I was feeling more distant and restless. Five children had been a huge focus for us, they had been such a part of our life and I am indebted to Di for her love and support in our life together. We made huge changes together, coming out and navigating a new way of living and bringing up children. It was me, in the end, who said I didn't want to carry on the relationship. It was devastating. We split up in the summer of 1995. I had known Di since 1979 when my youngest daughter was born, and we became lovers in 1982; so, we were together a long time. We are still good friends and I feel very lucky that Di is still in my life and we continue to maintain connections with our offspring.

I first met Anu in 1993, at a meeting in Bradford to organise a commemoration for Audre Lorde. I think what drew me to Anu was that her lifestyle was so different from mine. She lived in a caravan, was on the dole, lived very simply and was a lesbian separatist. Over the next couple of years, we saw each other at dyke events, but after Di and I split up we started going to see art exhibitions together, going for walks, going to the famous curry houses in Bradford and talking politics. We became lovers at the Winter Solstice in 1995. I was crazy in love with Anu and my life with her has remained alive all these years. We lived together for a few years, but it works much better for us to live independently. Our differences make our relationship strongly creative, loving and nurturing. Anu is my rock and I feel very blessed to share my old age with her.

In 2003 I became ill with chronic fatigue and fibromyalgia; some days I couldn't move from my bed without utter exhaustion. I felt I needed counselling for my spirit and I looked around for what was available. By chance I heard about the Coventina School of Shamanic and Creative Arts Therapy. I rang them; they were starting a two-year programme and they could send me the syllabus. It spoke to my dreams, bringing together counselling, ancient wisdoms, Nature as a teacher and healer, creativity and poetry. It was exactly what I craved and an amazing opportunity to explore another side of myself. I negotiated with the tutors to answer all the topics through creativity rather than essays, and they agreed. I found this process invaluable in understanding myself at a deeper level. For several years after that, I offered small workshops for women in shamanic healing through Nature. When we immerse ourselves in Nature, just being outside, we always get answers if we have a clear question.

Fundraising for women's groups

In 2012 Anu and I set up a group in Calderdale to fundraise for women's groups. There were eight lesbians involved in the initial group. We raised money for the annual Women in Tune music festival in Wales. (Their funding from the Lottery was withdrawn, as it was for all small community events, when money was diverted to the Olympics in 2012.) We continued fundraising year after year. The women in the initial group started doing different things and women have moved in and out. The group, now nine lesbians, has been together for several years and we now exclusively fundraise for LISG. We call ourselves the Valley Sisters; we work well together and LISG has come into our lives and enriched us in many ways, in awareness, connection and friendship.

The first time we organised a fundraiser for LISG was in October 2016. None of us had met anyone from LISG, but they came to the event – Karen S and about eleven members. It was very exciting, and also very moving, because a few of the women told their stories. You could have heard a pin drop.

A few weeks later, Karen S got in touch with me. She said there was a woman in LISG – it was Grace – who had been absolutely amazed at the fundraiser because there had been so many *older* lesbians there. She was older herself and she had been like, 'Are *all* these lesbians?'

Karen wondered if Grace could meet me and Anu, just for a bit of support. So we invited them over for lunch. Grace told us her story that day and I said I would be more than happy to write a letter of support for her in her ongoing case with the Home Office.

When I heard Grace's story, I was overwhelmed with the enormity of what the LISG women carry. To have to leave behind children, flee from families, friends, culture, language and their own country, solely for loving women, is unbearable. On top of all that, to find yourself in a country that is not welcoming... LISG welcomes! I wanted to be part of that welcoming. I had time; I could support in any way that would be helpful; I could learn. Anu and I both became volunteers. The twice-monthly meetings in Manchester were not Anu's thing, but she continued to support members going to court hearings and being there for individual women, as well as all the fundraising. I went to both volunteer and member meetings. It was a huge learning, because I didn't know anything about the asylum process. But, little by little, by reading, asking questions and just being there during the court hearings, I began to understand more.

I remember at one volunteer meeting when I asked how things worked between members and volunteers I was told, 'Well, it's an organic thing really.' I felt this response perfectly summed up the strength of LISG, a collective where all voices are encouraged and a collective that was open to different ways of working.

The members' meetings are such a bringing together of many voices, many backgrounds and cultures. It can feel chaotic and intense, but there is an overwhelming feeling of lesbians being together in this unique space.

Finding a role in LISG

I was a bit in awe of the other volunteers, particularly Karen S and Karen M, who were two of the three founders of LISG. And the other volunteers seemed to have such a lot of knowledge and experience, but they welcomed me and I knew I was in the right place.

It was Prossy who helped me find my role in LISG. We were in a volunteers' meeting, looking at individual women's cases. We were discussing how to support Grace, when Jane Traies's name came up, and her research and publications about older lesbians in the UK.

Prossy just turned to me. 'Couldn't you get in touch with Jane, Sorrel?'

And I said, 'Oh, okay.' I really hadn't a clue, I didn't have an email address or anything. But it was what I needed: a purpose. I found my feet and gradually my confidence grew. Since then Jane has used her knowledge and expertise to write several 'expert witness' letters based on her research.

Karen S so generously supported me. I shadowed her when talking one-to-one with women (with their permission), listening to their stories in order to write a support letter for their asylum claim with the Home Office. These meetings were harrowing and heartbreaking. On several occasions we were all crying. I began to focus more on letter writing as a way to support and on being there as a witness in court. Karen gave me feedback on my letters and I could always turn to her for information and support, knowing that she genuinely wanted to pass on her knowledge.

LISG feels like family. When a woman gets her leave to remain, all of LISG is euphoric: there is an outpouring of love, generosity and hope. It is humbling. It gives me a greater perspective about the world we live in.

SOPHIE

By contrast, Sophie is the youngest of our storytellers. Born in 1992, she was just twenty-seven at the time of our interview. 'At a very young age, I knew myself,' she says. A soccer-mad tomboy, she was always in danger of being recognised as a lesbian. So when she told me, 'The Home Office have rejected my claim – they don't believe I'm a lesbian,' I could only marvel that the officials were refusing to see the same signs, such as short hair and masculine clothing, that had worked against her in Namibia.

At fifteen, having lost both parents, Sophie was separated from her siblings and sent to live with an abusive uncle. When her sexuality was discovered, she was brutally punished for it – again, a story that is all too common. Sometimes it is hard to say how much of a woman's suffering has been because she is a lesbian and how much simply because she is a woman in a deeply misogynistic society. The abuse handed out to Sophie was bad enough before her sexual orientation was known, but it was much worse afterwards.

I lived with my uncle, on my own, and that was the life of hell. My uncle had a family, but he was a very abusive man, and his wife had divorced him; she took the kids and ran away. So I had to become his slave, and do everything for him. He just carried on being an abusing person; he even raped me. That's why I had to run away.

Where we come from, it's very hard to be a lesbian, and to open up about it, because typically, people don't like 'homos'. I knew already that I was a lesbian when I was about fifteen. When I was growing up, I used to spend most of the time with guys. I used to be playing soccer, wearing trousers... I mean, it was just more fun being with guys than being with girls. When I was with the girls, they'd be talking about their boyfriends, and I'm just thinking, 'What are you talking about?'

They'd be asking, 'Do you have a boyfriend?'

And I'd be like, 'Come on, I'm not having this,' and I'd always move to the guys' side. We'd be talking about soccer, and all that stuff. Then they'd be asking – you know how guys are – 'Oh, have you seen this girl?'

And I'd say, 'Yeah, I think she looks fine!'

So, at a very young age, I knew myself.

But it was hard, because I had to hide it. I even had to stop being friends with them, because my uncle was always asking me, 'Why do you like playing soccer?' and 'Why don't you wear skirts?' And I'd answer, 'It's just a sport that I used to do.'

So, most of the time after school I wouldn't be hanging out too much, I'd just be at home, and if I didn't do what he told me to do, then he'd be punishing me: for instance, I couldn't eat for a day, just take water; or he punished me by making me clean the yard in the sun. You come home from school and he says, 'You need to clean up this whole yard, pick up these old papers and do everything.' And you just have to do it.

First love

I started having something with a girl, and I told her I liked her. We'd just played a game of Spin the Bottle, and when the bottle stopped, the group said, 'You two, kiss!'

I said, 'No, why would I kiss her?'

And they were like, 'Come on, it's just a game, guys! Why are you going on about it?'

And I said, 'Okay, fine,' and I kissed her.

And next time she saw me, she kept on looking at me. Then she said, 'Can we have something together? But we must hide it.'

Because, where she came from, her father was kind of a chief, so such things wouldn't be allowed. And my uncle was also a very respected person, he used to be in the election to become a councillor, and the whole community looked up to him. And if a member of his family was to be gay, then it's going to be questionable, like, 'Why do you allow her to be like this?' That would be putting his reputation at risk.

So, it wasn't easy; we had to hide it. I'd meet up with this girl and we'd do our homework. I always had to say, 'Oh, at this time we have a lot of projects to do!' and sneak out to go and see her. And she did the same as well. That's how we used to see each other.

My uncle asked me, 'Why are you two always doing your homework together?'

I said 'We're in the same class, so we always get the same project. Our names follow each other's,' and all that stuff.

After a certain time, after two years, she had to end things, because her family, her sisters, were questioning her about it and becoming suspicious. She was getting afraid and knew that she was going to be in trouble if her father was to find out. At first, she just didn't want to tell me the truth. She told me she wasn't serious, she wasn't into women. I was very heartbroken, because I really did love her, and it was my first love, and it felt so good... but I just had to leave the whole idea. We wouldn't even see each other, or do homework together – and that's how it ended. She was the only girlfriend I had. Because of the suspicions of her sisters and all that, I became more afraid. What if I dated somebody else? I was afraid that if I moved to the next person, we might be found out.

'He read my diary'

When I was seventeen, two years after I went to live with my uncle, he went out drinking. When he came back, he was drunk, and he raped me. He threatened me not to report it or say anything. I understood, and I could do nothing. I just stayed with the guilt. I thought, 'Maybe it's my fault, maybe I did something to make him do that.'

Since I was on my own, I used to write everything in my

diary, all my feelings, even after breaking up with my girl-friend. 'Will I find somebody new? A girlfriend that I'll like?' I would always write it down, just like a person I'd talk to. I had a drawer in my room which was locked all the time, that's where I kept my diary and my other personal stuff. Maybe he got curious about why I kept on writing, what it was I kept on writing, I don't know. But one day, when I was still seventeen, I had a soccer match to go and play, and I nearly forgot my socks. They were in that same drawer, and when I took out the socks, because I was in a hurry, I dropped my notebook on the bed. And he was at home that day. I didn't know. I just said, 'Oh, I'll see you later,' and then I went. And he came in my room, and he found the book, and he read my diary.

When I came back, he was just sitting there. I took a shower, did my household cleaning and everything that I needed to do, and he was just sitting there. And the thing is, I found that book on the bed, and I was like, 'Shit. I hope he didn't go in it!' But it gave me the thought... and I took the book and put it back, but I was thinking, 'I just hope he didn't read it!'

But he was just quiet the whole time.

And then after that, when I went to bed, he came in my room. He told me that he was going to rape me, he was going to make me straight, he was going to make me like men, and he was going to lock me up. Either I would starve to death, or I would decide to change. So, he raped me that night as well, and then he locked me up for five days. He just gave me water.

'After five days, you have to change! I'm going to find you a man, and you're going to start dating men. This thing of you being a lesbian is not allowed!' So he locked me up and if he did give me food it would be stale, two days, three days old, that's the type of food he'd give me. He'd say, 'Here's something you need to eat for now, just so you have that energy for now, and don't die; but I also hope you die, and it's not going to be my fault.' He kept on telling me it's not his fault my parents died, he didn't kill my parents, it's because of their own stupidity that they died. Those are the sort of things he used to tell me all the time.

After five days, he actually just let me out. He went to work. He said, 'I hope that now you'll change, you'll start acting like a woman, you'll become a woman.'

Running away

He thought that I didn't have anybody else. But I had people, friends that I was talking to. So that's when I decided to run away. I went to a friend's place, though it wasn't really that far from my place. I stayed there, without coming out of the house. While I was staying there, maybe after five days, my friend told me that we should go and report this. I was frightened, and I knew that even if I reported it, they wouldn't do anything. When we reported it, they asked us, 'What kind of evidence do you have? If you say you were raped, why didn't you come that same day?' and that sort of thing. So the case was just dismissed, since it was my uncle, and he was somebody that they knew.

And then – I don't know if maybe the police told him, 'They came here to report you' – but, as I was walking in the street, I was attacked by five guys. They beat me up and they threatened me: 'If you don't change, next time we will rape you and we'll set you on fire, and you'll never live again. Just know that this is a warning.' They cut me – here, on my arm – I still have the mark. They used a sharp object to cut me, and they beat me, and they left me there. I don't know if they came from my uncle.

And that's when I decided to go. After I was attacked, I went to the hospital, and my friend said, 'Now you need to move from here. I will talk to my other friend, and you'll go and stay there. It's a bit further away. Don't go out during the day, and we'll look for a way to get you out of the country.'

When I ran away, I had a little money; I even had a phone. My uncle had a shop at home, and when I was living there, I used to work at his shop after school. Sometimes he'd pay me a little amount of money, sometimes nothing, because he'd say, 'You stay at my place, you eat my food, so you're not getting paid anything.' But every time he paid me that little amount, I would always save it, put it away and hide it. So I had some money. At night I used to go out (and I used to cover myself when I went out). I was selling old clothes that I wasn't wearing, and my friends used to give me their old clothes too. They'd give me things like crisps and sweets and whatnot, and they'd say, 'Just try to sell this stuff, just to make a little bit more money.' I had to save all that money. One of my friends decided, 'I have this laptop I'm not using, we're going to make just a little bit more money out of it, until we have enough for you to go, before you die. Because at the end of the day, he'll act as if he's not looking for you, but you don't know what he's going to do.'

I hadn't told my friends the reason why he attacked and raped me. They say that gay people, especially lesbians, are allowed in Namibia. Yes, it's legal, but they cannot provide protection for it. And if you decide to be like that, it's really hard. You can see other people that are really open about being lesbian, how they're being treated, how they're being abused, how they're being raped. You'd hear every day that somebody was raped, 'because you act like a man' or 'because he acts like a woman'. That whole thing just frightened me. I thought, 'If I have to live in this country, how will I open up to be me? I will have to change and live another person's life, just to satisfy everybody.' So I decided, maybe I will just go. If I have to go and die somewhere else, it's better than dying in my own country, at my own people's hands; it's worth it, giving it a try. Because I was tired, and I didn't know what to do. At night I wouldn't sleep, all these things kept on coming, so I'd just be there sitting, and I would not sleep until the sun came up.

The second friend I went to knew about an agency that sends people out of the country. He said, 'Before you die or lose your life, this guy must just send you anywhere you'll be safe.' So I didn't know exactly where he was going to send me. That guy who sends people told him, 'If you send somebody away, you just tell them to go and claim asylum. Anything that has happened to her, abuse or anything, she can just go and claim it, and then maybe she will be safe, since she was in a situation that she could not solve.'

They even helped me get my passport. Then they said, 'We can't let you go to a Namibian airport, so we'll use another way. You are going to have to go to South Africa.' I didn't know anybody in South Africa. I took a bus, but I didn't have enough money for the whole journey, so this person that I took the bus in with, he actually let me get in his car. He drove me a long way, then he told me that now maybe I should walk. It was many miles, because I had to walk almost a whole day to get to the airport. My flight was for the next day, so I slept at the airport. Then I got a plane from South Africa to the UK. I arrived at Manchester and I just claimed asylum there. That was in February last year, 2019.

People with golden hearts

The Home Office placed Sophie in a hostel in Liverpool for a while before moving her to Manchester. She was still attending an LGBT group in Liverpool (Many Hands One Heart) but was then given the number for LISG, and texted them saying she would like to join.

They gave me a date, saying, 'You can come and meet us then, and we can talk to you.' I met with one of the LISG volunteers and one of the members, and I talked to them. It wasn't easy, though. I mean, it was very hard to open up and tell somebody the whole story.

I love LISG. It's a nice group; that's where I met a lot of people, a lot of friends. These people have golden hearts. It was so hard. I mean, I'm a person like this, I keep myself on my own, I'm used to being quiet, I don't like communicating. I just like being on my own, because of what happened to me. As I was starting to open up, it was very hard, because I used to think that people could feel or see what had happened to me. But then I've got these nice people in LISG, people that are willing to help, people that are willing to listen, and I made a lot of friends, and I love LISG. Every time they say, 'There's this event,' I always want to go!

At first it was a bit too hard for me, because I wasn't really myself, still broken. But I'm fighting it. I'm seeing this counsellor, from the GP. It is helping me. I still don't sleep, because sometimes I have those flashbacks, where those things are happening, and I get frightened, I get nervous, I think of dying, maybe. But I'm getting counselling, and I'm getting some pills just to help me sleep at night. I didn't go to Rape Crisis yet, but I need to go there, too.

Still waiting

The ways are different here, and at first it was too odd. In the winter, it is so, so cold! But I think I'm better off, far from my own country. Because even if things are so hard, I'm not being beaten, I'm open, I'm free. Nobody says anything like, 'Why are you wearing clothes like a man?' That's the good thing. And people are more friendly, people are more smiling and willing to help. At first, I couldn't even ask a person, 'Where is this shop?' At first, it was very hard to do this, but when you get to know, people are willing to help you. So, I prefer being here to being at home.

The Home Office have rejected my claim. They don't believe I'm a lesbian. So now I'm appealing against that. I have a solicitor and I'm still waiting for the hearing date. When I get my stay, I would love to study, first of all. I want to do something with IT, perhaps IT engineering. Something that is just with computers. I do like communicating with people, but I'd rather stress my mind over computers than people. I want to get my own place, and I'd be willing to volunteer with LISG. I mean, it's a nice thing... That's what I'd also want to do.

~

Sophie's appeal was heard just a few weeks after our interview, in March 2020 – one of the very last hearings at Manchester before the Covid-19 pandemic closed the courts. This time, the judge, persuaded by the evidence from LISG, did agree that she was, after all, a lesbian. Sadly, that wasn't the end of the story: the judge decided it was safe, even so, for Sophie to return to Namibia. So now she has to fight that decision, too, in order to remain in the UK.

CHIPO

Although every woman's story is unique, there are some themes that recur time and again. The next storyteller, Chipo, was taught from childhood that homosexuality was a sin; a combination of Christian teaching and society's disapproval convinced her that what she felt was deeply wrong. This internalised homophobia is a burden carried by many of the contributors to this book, whether their religious background is Christian, Muslim or another, traditional belief. Chipo was also under intense pressure from her family to marry – a pressure she could not, in the end, escape – and she describes the restrictions and misery of her marriage to a man she barely knew. Her loneliness in this emotionally abusive relationship is echoed in other women's stories, too.

Chipo's journey to freedom was exhausting and terrifying; but she believed that, once she reached the UK, all would be well. She was shocked when she began to understand the struggle that still lay ahead of her. The complexity (and, often, the apparent callousness) of the Home Office's asylum process is another theme that recurs frequently in this book. It would be hard enough for a fluent English speaker with a good income and robust mental health to negotiate the twists and turns of asylum law: almost always, the person seeking asylum has none of those advantages. As you will see, Chipo is a strong, determined woman and was finally granted leave to remain in the UK. Now she is studying, aiming to make a career for herself, and also working with LISG as they support other women like her.

I'm one of six children – it's an average family size in Zimbabwe – and I'm the second. I've got an older brother, and then younger sisters. I grew up in a Christian area of Bulawayo, so although it's a big city, in that district we knew each other very well. Zimbabwe is mainly Christian, but some of the people believe in other cultural traditions. I went to an ordinary school, but during assembly time we'd be singing Christian songs, and we'd pray before we started our day, so it was a school that held Christian values.

Where I grew up, I was expected to be in a relationship with guys; but when I was nineteen, after high school, that's when I started to have those contradictory feelings. Boys were interested in me; they were showing a lot of interest, buying me chocolates, sweets and stuff, but I was a bit confused, thinking, 'What's going on?' Because I knew what I was feeling, and that it was totally unacceptable. Sometimes I felt, 'It's impossible!' I felt very bad about it, I knew it was wrong. I grew up in a very strict Christian family and I knew that it was very wrong. At the same time, when I was at high school, you were told to stay away from boys. It was, 'If you make a mistake, you'll fall pregnant,' and all that. Then, after high school, 'You need to get married and have a family!' But I wasn't feeling like it. I had a relationship with this one boy; it was okay in the beginning, but still I didn't feel a connection. My friends were doing it; my friends were getting love letters – it wasn't like now, when we have phones – so we'd exchange the letters, and it was, 'I've got these!' I just went along with it, but it didn't feel right with me. There was no attraction at all.

'One fateful day'

I *was* attracted to my best friend at that time, but she didn't know. It was difficult. Even for those who knew, who had already come out, it was difficult to approach someone, because you weren't sure how the person would react. Until, one fateful day… She used to sleep over at mine, I would sleep over at hers, and – it just happened! It confirmed a lot of things I'd been feeling, but I felt fear at the same time. I felt shame. I think she wasn't too sure how I would react, and I wasn't sure either. What was going to happen? Was she going to say something? Would I also say anything? We went on for a long time just like that, until one big mistake that I made. I told my cousin.

I think it was out of excitement, like, 'Okay, I like her,

she likes me, and we get along well, and it's more than just a friendship!'

So that was the mistake I made, and my cousin was like, 'What? That's not right!'

And she told my mum.

I denied everything. I just said, 'No, she didn't hear well,' and this and that.

After that, my cousin wasn't comfortable with me any more. Nothing in me had changed, I was still myself, but she wasn't comfortable any more. We still shared a bed, we still spent time together, but I felt more like a stranger to her.

Time to get married

This went on until I was twenty-one, when I was officially told, 'You can get married now, you can be with whoever you want.' But it didn't happen. Twenty-two, it didn't happen; twenty-three, it didn't happen.

In our culture, they always send our aunties to talk to us. (Like, 'Just find out. Is there a problem? What's going on? Is she okay?') So, my auntie asked me, 'What's going on? You're beautiful, we're still waiting for you to get married!'

I'd say, 'It's not happening, no one is chasing after me.'

But it was unbelievable. Twenty-five, twenty-six... They couldn't take it any more, especially my father.

After I left school, I was just at home. I didn't go to work. I was doing a little bit of hairdressing, but I couldn't further my studies. My dad was very strict. My mum was very understanding but, unfortunately, she was somebody who had to go along with the culture. She just wanted us to do whatever we would want; but at the same time, she could not speak out. Women in Zimbabwe, we can't speak like men. You don't have a word; you don't have a say. My father was not working any more: he had retired, so he was also home most of the time. I was the first-born daughter; he was expecting someone to marry me, and looking at a bride price. We have that thing called a bride price: when you get married the husband has to pay. Traditionally they have to bring cows but, in the city, it's converted to money. So they can say, 'Oh, for our daughter you need to pay about seven cows,' and if one cow is a hundred pounds, this means you have to pay seven hundred pounds. If you have a girl, it's a fortune. So, when girls were growing up, the parents would be looking forward to having that. My mum told me, when she was growing up, she and her sisters were never allowed to go to school. My grandfather was looking for them to get married, and only the boys, only my uncles, were educated. It carried on with us, except that, when it came to our generation, we were allowed to go to school, but we were still expected to get married.

So my dad started to invite these guys from church, started to compliment some boys. 'Oh, that boy, he's well behaved, he's like this...' He would invite them home for tea, and I'd have to serve them and give them food. Then they'd invite somebody different. All of them were attracted to me, but I would always find a way of saying no. Until they couldn't take it any more, so they sat me down and my auntie told me that somebody had come asking for my hand in marriage.

I said, 'I'm not ready yet.'

But they said, 'There's no way you cannot be ready, at twenty-six! One way or another it has to be done. We've accepted him, he's coming, it's So-and-so.'

And 'So-and-so' was about ten, fifteen years older than me; but he was well off. So that was it. They came, they brought everything that was supposed to be brought for the family, and then we were told, 'You need to know each other.' I'd been talking to him, I knew him from church, but not on a relationship level. So I was taken there and there was a celebration, with a traditional part where my auntie and my two cousins took me to theirs: they welcomed me, they did a party.

A married woman

It was not good. No. He was proud, he was showing off, he'd got somebody young, beautiful. And I didn't have a child, then. They always consider that means you've been taking good care of yourself, because most girls of my age, they were having kids, but I was at home, not having any. So, for the first few days, for him I was a trophy. To me, it felt more like I'd just have to be there, and make him happy whichever way I had to, to do whatever. I had to act like a married woman, now.

As time went on, I used to go and see my family, especially my aunties, and I would tell them that I wasn't happy. I couldn't say that I had feelings for women. No. I was just telling them how I was being treated in my marriage. So I'd always get advice: 'Oh, men are like that, so you need to behave this way...' They'd give me advice and tips on how to behave, how to carry myself. 'No, you need to do this, you need to do that!' But I was feeling that I wished I had just been given a moment to explore my feelings first, to find out if I was okay with it or not. I just wished I'd had a platform to experience, to satisfy my curiosity, to decide, 'Oh, maybe it's just...'

Within a short time, I fell pregnant. But before that he had started to limit me, to go out less, to dress in a certain way, like a married woman. I needed to put on a long skirt below my knees, to cover my hair all the time. He needed to come home and find a fresh cooked meal, house clean, clothes ironed. I needed to cut down on friends, I didn't need friends. So there started to be rules. I would say, 'I can't do that.' It was the first time I'd been married, and I thought I was allowed to have friends; I thought I would be allowed to go home! But even if I did go home, my mum would say, 'Time's up, you need to go, your husband will be coming back soon.' Even my dad would be asking, 'When are you going back?' I could feel that I didn't have my space any more at home, it wasn't there. I was just treated like a visitor, and I was given a time limit when I'd got to go. I could see the sadness in my mum's face; I feel sure she understood what I was going through, but she was voiceless. She could not say anything. She could not decide, but she could see. She could tell.

I gave birth to a daughter. I had a bad time giving birth and, afterwards, I wasn't much attached to her. When I was still at the hospital, I was diagnosed with post-traumatic stress after giving birth; that's what they said it was. So I wasn't too attached to her; I wasn't ready for a child. But as time went on, and it was only me and her, I started to learn to love her. She was the only one who gave me happiness and smiles, in all that misery. So, slowly, we had a bond. We were okay.

But the fighting at home was just going on and on. I think that he had paid all the dowry that was wanted by my family, and didn't owe even a penny. (Sometimes, people maybe pay half, but he had paid it all.) So it was just a reminder, every day, 'Oh, I paid this, I paid this, I feel like I've wasted my money. You need to behave like this, you need to act like this, because I've done this for your family, I don't owe them anything, you're my wife!' And things like that. We'd fight a lot. We'd fight to a point where I couldn't take it any more. We would fight, and then the police would come. I'd explain what was happening, he would have his side of the story, and they would just say, 'Oh, you need to go home and sort this out. You need to have your elders sit you down and talk about this, and fix your problems. This is nothing. Blah, blah, blah...'

Until the final point, where we fought and I told him, 'I didn't know you! To me, this was just an arranged thing. Yes, I knew you from church, we'd talk, we'd do this and that, but not on an intimate level. And with me, I feel like I love women!'

Yeah. I said that. It was just out of anger, out of frustration. Because I would not rest – even if I hadn't had feelings for women, with the way he was treating me, I just didn't feel – there was no connection at all. I felt like I was an object.

So that was a big fight, and the police came, and the police now were interested about what I'd said. Did I say it?

Knowing the police, I said, 'No, I didn't say that.'

And he's saying, 'Yes, she said that.' And it was an issue.

'That was why I had to leave my country'

I went back to my parents, with my child. He would come, and he would swear and shout insults. He'd be coming and tormenting them, wanting his money back that he'd paid, wanting this and that. He would scream; he would just stand outside and shout, and cause a scene. And my dad felt embarrassed then. But I couldn't go back, I just couldn't. I said I'd just go and wander, I didn't know where, but would never go back there. Then, in 2009, my dad passed on, and I was just with my mum. Things were a bit lighter, then. She had her suspicions about me, but at the same time I'm her daughter, and I think that now the tough men had gone, she had that soft spot for me and the child. So we were okay, we were fine.

Then I started to try and socialise, and go out with friends and so on, and that is when I met this lady. I was doing someone's hair, and she said, 'I'm having a party tomorrow in my house!' She invited me, so I went. We had drinks, with a few friends, and that was how I met this lady. That was why I had to leave my country. Yes! She was the reason.

At that time, in our culture, it was very rare for women to wear trousers. My dad wouldn't allow us to wear trousers. Even if we were going for sports, okay, we'd take our sports kit, but when we'd leave home we were dressed in our skirts. So, I used to put on my dresses. Then I met this lady at the party: she was in jeans and I could see she was comfortable. I wasn't comfortable, because that's something I was not used to.

So we just had a chat, and we spoke about relationships, and I was like, 'Are you seeing someone?'

'No.'

'Married?'

'No.'

'Okay.'

And then I said, 'I'm not married. I don't think I'll be married.'

And she said, 'Why?'

'I don't think I will be.' And I asked her, and she said the same thing.

But we were laughing all the time when we were talking about not getting married, and not having a reason, so there was something that clicked between the two of us. I was thinking, 'What's going on?' But neither of us could say. And she couldn't tell me why.

We just had a good time. Then, later on, after a few drinks, she said, 'No, I'm into women.'

'*Really?*'

'Yes.'

And it's a conversation that is rare, that is difficult. For someone to open up, and then it just happens that you're *both* like that! The chances are about two out of ten. Because no one trusts anyone. But she trusted me, and I trusted her as well, and we carried on all night, just talking together.

I was about to go, but the lady who had invited me said, 'I've got spare rooms, you can all sleep here. You don't have to worry about going back home. Your mum would not approve of alcohol.'

And I agreed. 'No, I'm too drunk, I can't go home.'

The lady I had just met said the same excuse. So we had a room. And then... what happened, happened!

And we went to sleep. We'd left the other guys still partying. During the party, some guys started to fight; they were fighting downstairs over a girlfriend. We didn't know what happened, and we were not even interested, but that's when the police came in. And they found us there.

That's when the trouble started. Even today, I don't know what happened downstairs, but the police found us there, in that awkward position. There was no way I could deny that I was a lesbian, when they found us naked!

Things were just all over the place, because we'd been tipsy. I was trying to dress, and one of the police officers was saying, 'No, don't dress up, we need evidence. We need evidence, so that you'll go to the police station and explain why we find you together like that.'

I was trying to cover myself up, and one was saying, 'Cover up! Get dressed!' and the other one was saying, 'No, don't!'

My girlfriend was trying to protect me. She was more muscular than me – I was very tiny, I was size eight then, I think – and he said to her, 'Oh, so you're the man! We'll show you!'

And they hit her, very hard, right in front of me.

My girlfriend passed out. She lost consciousness.

The officers told me to get cold water in a bucket so they could throw it on her, so she would wake up. I went outside to get water (our taps are always outside). I didn't put on my shoes, I was just half dressed, and as I was opening the tap I thought, 'No one is watching me... let me just go!' I felt guilty about leaving her, but at the same time I didn't know where they would take me, what they would do to me, after witnessing what they did. And I was scared. So, just behind the house, I jumped over the fence and ran off. I couldn't go home, so I went to one of the pastors of our local church.

I just said, 'They found me sleeping with my friend, and this is what they're saying, they're saying this and this. So I need a place to sleep, because if I go home, they will trace me home, and I won't be safe.'

He said, 'No, I can't keep you here either, because if they

find you here, I'll also be in trouble.' He gave me eighty dollars and said, 'Here is money, where do you think you can go?'

I said I could go to other members of my family. But then I thought, 'I'm going to South Africa. That's it. I'm not going to stay here.'

I just left. I went to a place I knew about – it's like a bus station, where they pick up people who are going to South Africa, with or without a passport. A lot of young people, after school, go there. It's popular. I went straight there, and I said to the guys, 'I want to go to South Africa.'

The man said, 'Okay, where are you going?'

'Jo'burg.'

He said, 'Where in Jo'burg?'

I didn't know. So I just said, 'When I get there, I'll phone my relatives.' But I didn't really have anyone there.

They said, 'Okay.' And they took me.

A terrifying journey

It took about eleven hours. Just before we got to the border, they said, 'Everyone get off who doesn't have a passport!' And this guy said, 'We've got to walk a short distance, then we'll meet them.'

I had told them, 'I don't have a passport with me,' and they had said, 'Oh, it's fine, we'll take you there.' But I didn't know how we would have to get there. We had to get out and walk in the bushes all the way to the South African border.

We came to a river, the Limpopo. When we saw it, we said, 'Oh my God, this is a big river!'

He said, 'We are going to go in and cross that river. Don't walk slowly, because there are crocodiles.'

They didn't tell us until we got there. Some other guys they had working with them said, 'Yes, there are crocodiles here, you need to walk fast.'

We had to hold each other, like a train. If you were just too slow, they would leave you; they'd already taken the money, so whether you go or you stay, they wouldn't lose anything.

It was horrible. It was so horrible. My feet!

Then when we got out of the river, the distance that we had to walk! It took about three and a half hours, walking and hiding, hearing sounds... There were police patrolling the borders, so we'd hide, we'd dive and keep quiet, and then, 'Okay, let's go!' and we'd walk again, until we got to the other side, into South Africa, where we met our transport.

That cost sixty dollars, so I was left with twenty. I didn't know where I was going, I didn't know anybody in that place. I just knew I couldn't have stayed at home, I had to leave. The morning after we arrived, one of the drivers took me to a refugee centre run by the Methodist Church. There were a lot of people there from different countries; they'd go there to sleep and get food, and then during the day they'd all roam around, and in the evening go back there. It was overcrowded. The people there told us we needed to go to another city, like Pretoria, where refugees could register. But at that time there was an outbreak of xenophobia – South Africans were killing foreigners – and it wasn't safe to travel.

I approached one of the volunteers. I told her what I'd been through and what my situation was. She said there was an NGO organisation in Jo'burg I could go to. She said, 'I'll get the contacts for you and you can go there and talk to them, and hear what they suggest.' I was still not sure if I was safe. So when we went there (I think they were from the US, they were running some charitable organisations in South Africa), I told them everything. And they said, 'Okay, we'll see how we can help you. If you go to Europe, you'll be safe as an LGBT person, because they take care of people like you.'

It took about three or four days before they managed to organise a travelling document for me: I gave them the money and they booked me a flight. And they said, 'Wherever you get off, at whichever airport, just tell them that this is where you're coming from, and this is who you are. Just let them know straight away, and they'll help you.' I didn't know the difference between the UK, the US, Italy or whatever. I just knew I was going to Europe, to a safe place.

'Even more horrible'

But when I got here, that's when I discovered, 'Oh, my God, it's going to be even more horrible!'

I think in my mind I'd thought that, once I get here, that's it. I'll only have to explain myself. I'd trusted those people. Because they were white, and it was a big organisation, I took their word for it. I thought, 'Okay, if they say it's like this, then it's magic.' But the journey I took when I was here – the journey of claiming asylum, going through the process – was even more traumatising.

I think it was London where I arrived. I told them I wanted to claim asylum and they put me aside with three or four other people who'd come from different places – there were two who I think were Asian, and myself and another lady. Then they took us to a hotel not far from the airport, where they took all our details. The following day, they drove us to Croydon. At Croydon, there was a short interview, where they want to know about how you got there, where you are from, what happened. It was really short, I think about forty minutes. This was in the morning, and then we were told to wait the whole day while they found a place for us. They were supposed to take us to Liverpool, where there's a centre for refugees. We waited the whole day and they said, 'Oh, it's full.' Then they booked us into a hotel not too far from Croydon. We all shared with other people. I think we were there four days.

Then the following day, they took us to Wakefield, where I stayed about three months. Now they were explaining where we were and how the process works: that you need to find a solicitor and explain your story, and they'll take you to court, and you start the process there. They gave us solicitors from around that area, immigration solicitors. We were waiting for accommodation. After three months, I was given accommodation, and then I had to change my solicitor because it was in a different place.

That's when the process really started for me; but, at the same time, I still didn't understand what was going on. I was a bit traumatised as well, and stressed about everything. I couldn't sleep, I couldn't cope… and the weather! It was August when I got here, and the weather got worse. And it was hard trying to blend in, in the community, finding my way. So I went to my GP, and they referred me to a counsellor. I started going for counselling.

Then I went to see a solicitor. I had my interview at the Home Office. It was six or seven hours long. They wanted to know everything: 'When did you start to feel like a lesbian? When did you start to feel those feelings? How did you live?' Everything that I went through, my marriage, everything. It felt just horrible. Because I didn't expect it… it was really horrible. And then the court…

They sent a refusal. The reason for the refusal was that they didn't believe I was a lesbian. That was the main argument, that I was not lesbian.

'Completely on my own'

At that time, I had not started going to the church, I had not known about LISG, so I was completely on my own. We went to court, and I didn't have anyone with me, I was just by myself. I didn't know other people; I hadn't made friends. So I was just lost. And going into court, if you've never done it, it's a big thing. The judge was male, my solicitor was male, the Home Office person was male. And the questions they were asking! 'Oh, when did you feel you were gay? What made you think it? Maybe it was just a stage?' And then, 'Were you really sexually abused? How did it happen?' Coming from Africa, we are so reserved, there are some things you can't say, and at that time I didn't know that the things I was *not* saying were what would have won my case! I was shy and nervous, and not knowing what's right to say and what's right not to say. You have to re-walk every traumatic experience, you need to say it and describe it as it is. But I think I held a lot of it in.

The solicitor said, 'Oh, we need to appeal.' So we appealed. Then, after a few weeks, the judge said, 'Oh, we accept that she's gay, but we don't believe she was sexually abused and things like that, and we don't believe what she said happened to her, she has failed to prove that it is unsafe for her to return to Zimbabwe.' So that's how it was dismissed.

With legal aid, once it's dismissed like that, they lose interest. My solicitor said, 'I won't carry on with you, you need to find another solicitor, you need to do a fresh claim.' At that time, I didn't even know what a 'fresh claim' was, or what they were expecting of me; because I had told them all I knew, I'd given them my all. And then a few weeks after that refusal, they sent a letter saying, 'You need to leave the place where you live,' because I had exhausted my claim.

Sometimes, I feel like the Home Office deal with just a number of immigrants, they don't take into considera-tion that we are human beings. Because if they did that, and thought of the families who are left behind, I think people would be treated in a more humane manner than just a number. Especially women. If they say, 'Oh yes, this is happening, we believe what happened to this person,' then why are they treating them the same way here? Why would you leave a vulnerable woman homeless? Why would you do that? Knowing Britain is a charitable country, I've always said that they are good at giving, they've got a good heart; but when it comes to that particular subject, the doors are shut. I think women should be treated in a different way. Even if the cases fail, I think that to offer them shared accommodation, or just a centre where they know they won't be out on the street, it would be something.

I left my accommodation. I didn't have anywhere else to go, so on the day the housing officer came, I left my luggage there and the girls I'd been sharing with said, 'Oh, you can come back and sleep at night.' So I would just wander around, and go back there to sleep. Then, at the food bank where I was going, they told me, 'You can go to Manchester, there is a homeless place there, ask them for accommodation.' I went to Manchester and found the place, where you also need to walk around during the day and then at night you go and sleep. But it's mixed, and there's all these drug addicts that are on the street, and you are so scared and terrified.

Help at last

I was still going for counselling, and I told the lady what was happening. She contacted Manchester Rape Crisis, and they gave me the contact for LISG, and for First Wednesday, and the Metropolitan Church. They are the people that took over and helped me while I was preparing my case. They were the ones that explained to me, 'Actually, this is what they're looking for, this is what you have to do now.' They worked with me to build up the case, and to apply for new accommodation.

I started to attend the Metropolitan Church and I used to have a lot of questions. I think when I came here, I still lived in guilt. I still had that guilt because there were scriptures that were being quoted – the most popular one was that Sodom and Gomorrah were destroyed because of homosexuality. So it's the scriptures that we grew up knowing, that have been planted in our minds, telling us that it's not right. Even if your feelings are telling you otherwise, deep down in your heart you feel guilty. It's torture, you feel bad. Because of what you've been believing all your life, you also want to get married and have kids and have a man who'll take care of you.

So, when I started attending that church, I used to talk a lot with the pastor there. I'd ask him, 'I want to understand, what did the Bible mean about this?' And he would give me a totally different explanation. And it made sense.

I'd say, 'But this is what I grew up knowing.'

He'd say, 'No, this is what it means. The Bible says, "Love your neighbour as you love yourself," and it says we should not judge. If this is what you say you are, I should not be the judge.'

So I started to feel different and loosen up. I started to understand, and tried to take myself away from guilt and from feeling like that.

And meeting other women in LISG, women shared the same stories. You know, sometimes somebody's pain can heal you, and then you'll be like, 'Okay, we'll get on with it.' Even meeting some women here, when I was going through counselling and stuff, meeting some British women who are rape survivors, gave me a positive mind. Because sometimes when you're going through bad things, all you feel is, 'It's only me! Why me?' – not knowing that other people are also going through stuff like that. Some things, you don't know how they're done, but when we meet at LISG, we talk, we make friends, and we manage to cheer each other up.

So, when I went to court the last time, when I got my stay, I wasn't on my own. My court was so full! It was packed. And just to know that there are people who support you and understand you, even if they're not saying anything, who are just there. It gives comfort, and it makes you more coura-geous. So I was not nervous like I was before. I just needed that support. I always feel bad for people who don't have the support, who don't know about this organisation, LISG. Because I also didn't know! And then you'd be on your own.

There were a lot of petitions last year, a lot of complaints about how the Home Office deal with LGBT cases, because they're not at all sympathetic; and, you know, they're sensitive cases. Like in my case, according to the law of Zimbabwe it's not illegal to be a lesbian, though it's illegal for gay men. There's a meeting at the LGBT Foundation, the First Wednesday, and it's men and women who are LGBT from different countries, so I've met a lot of Zimbabwean gay men. When they come here, they get their stay straight away. It's so simple, because that's what the law says. But because you are a woman, because this is what the law says, they don't consider the danger you are in. But I'm coming from a patriarchal country, where a woman is nothing. So, if something can get a man killed, what about a woman? I'm working closely with LISG now, so we'll see this year how the Home Office are treating women's cases.

Starting to think of the future

Asylum-seeking people are not allowed to work, but now I have my status, I want to build a future. I would love to do social work. I'm studying for GCSE English and maths, but I'm struggling with the maths! If I don't do social work, I'd like to do support work or working with vulnerable women, domestic violence, or whatever. But first, English and maths – this June.

My mum has always been there for me. After I left Zimbabwe, I would write to my mum and she would write back. I think everything changed when I left. I was the breadwinner at home; I was taking care of them, with the little that I would get. After I left, they struggled a lot. For a long time, she would always say, 'Oh, we're okay,' until at some point my daughter was not feeling too well, and she just had to open up and tell me about my daughter being ill. At those moments I was so stressed, and I could not tell her what I was going through here. My daughter was five when

I left, so now she must be ten. She is the main reason why I kept on fighting. Even when things got difficult here in this country, having her in my mind just gave me the strength. We talk on the phone, but there is still not that bond. She's closer to my mum than to me. So now, I'm trying to apply for her to come and join me. I hope she can. I do hope so.

AZANAT

Although unprepared for their long struggles with the Home Office, both Sophie and Chipo understood enough about the asylum process to know that they must claim asylum as soon as they arrived in the UK. Azanat's position was very different. She had come to England from Nigeria with her husband, and at that stage had never thought of claiming asylum. So when she ran away from him, she had nowhere to go and no idea how to find help. She was reduced to sleeping in a railway station. The turning point in Azanat's story comes with an act of kindness from a stranger – a passing commuter with a compassionate heart.

Unusually among the contributors, Azanat's asylum process was comparatively short, because the evidence she submitted to the Home Office was so compelling. But, as so many of these stories show, the mental and emotional challenges do not end with 'getting your stay'. The legacy of abuse can be long-lasting. As Prossy says later in this book, 'After I got my status, I had to face things, you know? What you've been through, you have to face it. So hard.' Azanat and many other LISG women are now receiving support from relevant organisations, but it can be a long, gruelling journey.

I'm the seventh child out of nine. I'm the only child of my mother, because my father has six wives: I'm from a polygamous Muslim family. I wasn't ever attracted to boys at all; I don't see any attraction in boys. When I was ten years old, I went to a girls-only high school, not far from where I lived. I'm only attracted to girls. I didn't have breasts very soon, but I saw other girls who were growing, and I'm always fond of touching... so gradually, gradually... There was a girl I really liked. Her name was Idayat. She was very passionate about me as well, and when we went to school, at assembly time I'd always secure a place for her to stand. That was how I began to know I was interested in girls. But where I grew up, because my parents are Muslim, we'd go for Quranic lessons. It says in the Quran that it's an abomination for girls to touch girls; it's an abomination for boys to touch boys. So, in those days, when I was feeling that way with Idayat, I was always unhappy. I felt it was wrong, I felt ashamed of it, I wanted to get my mind off it. It was very hard. I couldn't tell anybody.

Shamed and punished

I remember when we had our first kiss. Idayat was my first girlfriend, and that was my first kiss. It was in 1997, when I was fourteen years old. Before then, we'd only been very close friends. Because she was smart, sometimes she'd help me out with my homework. We didn't live in the same area; when I walked home, her parents would come and pick her up. So I didn't get to know her house, but we were always very close in school. In school we had rules as well, for girls not to touch girls; they taught us that in school, as well as what they taught me from the Quran. It was always like that.

But when I had those feelings towards her – it was in February 1997 – I wrote on a piece of paper, 'I am passionate about you!' and she replied that she had a passion towards me! (I didn't say it in English – my language then was Yoruba.) So I wrote this letter, that was how it began. And we kissed, and we were always looking for a reason to meet up.

We were caught one day, in the toilets, and that was the beginning of a horrible life in Nigeria. They called an emergency assembly – they rang a bell so everyone would come – and we were shamed in front of everybody. We were told to call our parents; and even before we went home, we were beaten by the superiors.

My mum said, 'What happened?' and I couldn't tell her.

I just said, 'You need to come to the school.'

She asked my dad, and he said, 'You can go.'

So, when she came to the school, they told her everything.

They told her that Idayat and I were being expelled.

When I got home and my dad heard about it, I was beaten again. They put fresh pepper in my private parts. Hot pepper. I can never forget that day.

After my mum did that to me, my dad beat me, too. He was shouting, 'This is demonic! Where did you get this kind of thing from?' Because of this ill-treatment from my mum and dad, I felt so ill, they took me to hospital and I spent a week there. Then I came back home. I stayed at home for a month, then my dad registered me at another school, which was a mixed school. When I wasn't at school I was being monitored. I couldn't see Idayat again and I felt heartbroken. But I felt it would be okay, because I'd be a normal person. My mum and dad took me to a cleric, to pray for me, so that I would not feel that way any more. I was prayed over, and they would do some Islamic thing... I was being really monitored. After I finished at that school, my dad said he wouldn't let me do any further study, so I went to live with my grandmother. It's really far from where my parents are. I moved in with my grandmother, and I was there for about a year.

'Something dropped into my heart'

In Nigeria, there is not running water in every house, except for the rich people; there's always a well. There was a borehole not far from where my grandmother used to live and I normally went there to fetch water. And that's where I met my second girlfriend. When I was in secondary school, I thought, 'I will change!' I really felt that I could change – but when I met Chidinma, and she helped me lift the water to carry on my head, something just dropped into my heart and I felt something. I tried to shy away from it all. I felt, 'No, this shouldn't happen again! I don't want this to happen to me again.'

She asked where I lived, and I said, 'Oh, I live down

the road. I live with my grandmother. I've just finished at school.'

She lived nearby as well. She also lived with her grand-parents, and her brothers lived there with her.

We just chatted for a few minutes and then we went our ways.

So, every other day, we'd go there and we would meet at the well, and we'd talk. We'd talk about girls... she didn't really talk about boys, though there were always boys as well as girls coming to the borehole. And something in me said, 'I'm not the only one. There is nothing wrong with me. There is another person who is just like me!'

She told me I could come to her house. Our grandparents, they were all religious fanatics, and they had this Quranic session in their house in the evenings, so I'd just tell my grandmother, 'I'm going to Chidinma's,' and she'd normally allow me.

In the morning, if I wanted to see her, I'd pour all the water away, so I could go and get more water. And my grandmother would say, 'You just fetched water two days ago! Why do you want more?'

And I'd say, 'It's finished.'

'What did you do?'

'Oh, I've been cleaning the house...' and all that. Just to go and see her.

And she too, sometimes she'd come to my grandmother's and we'd walk and talk. And so it started. We didn't really say, but we just felt the same way.

'An abomination'

Then her brother caught us. From here on, it was a really, really horrible time, as well. We were in Chidinma's room. He opened the door. And he said, 'This is a Muslim house! Abomination, abomination, abomination!'

And he called people on us, and we were taken to the

police station. And I'm telling you, this was the day I said, 'This religion is not a good religion.' Because they were fanatical Muslims.

They took us to the police station, and even at the police station, me and Chidinma were molested by the policemen. We were molested.

They didn't come and fetch us that day. The police sent for them to fetch me, but they did not come. When I asked to talk to my grandmother, they said, 'No, she doesn't want to listen.'

In those days, there were no mobile phones. So my grandma sent for my parents to come and get me, and after a week they came, and heard what had happened, again.

My dad said, 'This is not right! This is really an abomination.'

I was taken to a Muslim place and told to recite the Quran. But this time I felt different about it. I thought, 'This is me. You can't change me. I've tried to change, but this is me.' And by this time, I was more mature. But it is an abomination to my religion, and in society, too – because when Chidinma and I were caught, all around that area everyone, even the politicians, were saying, 'Why would you like girls? You should like men!'

And, of course, it's illegal.

I went back to my parents, and this time round, I was under really strict monitoring. I would go out to the market in the morning with my mum and we'd come back home together in the evening. She didn't allow me to be on my own, or ever to have a female friend. She was a trader, and when people came to her shop to buy groceries, if men were trying to make advances to me, or crack jokes with me, and I didn't respond properly, my own mother would slap me. 'What's wrong with you? He's talking to you. Talk back to him!'

One horrible day, the first day of January 2004, because they are Muslims they went to pray. I was not clean – when you have your menstrual period you are not allowed to go to the mosque – so I stayed at home. When my parents were at the mosque with my older brothers, some men came into the house, and I was raped. It wasn't just one person, it was four men, and one of them was saying, 'We know you are a lesbian. We will make you straight!' I couldn't do anything – I tried to pull myself away, but I was beaten. One of them was holding my mouth, one was ripping my clothes off...

When my parents came back, they wouldn't pity me. Even my own mother wouldn't pity me. They saw what had happened. They asked me, and I said, 'Men came to the house.'

Then they said, 'Shut up!'

My mum said, 'Shut up, I don't want to hear anything!'

They didn't take me to the hospital; no treatment, nothing. And I was told never to tell anyone about this. They couldn't take me to the police station, because I'd already had an issue with the police from years back. So, I couldn't tell anyone. I was silenced. Even today, I'm still going through post-traumatic stress because of that. Sometimes when I think about it, I feel horrible... I've been to Rape Crisis and I've been to Think Ahead – Think Ahead is helping me. For the past twelve weeks, I've been going and it's been helping me. They said that I *can* deal with it, and leave it, and go forward.

'My kind of woman'

It was like that for years. I was still living at home, but I went to study fashion design; and I found another friend. Her name was Oyinye. By that time, I was more mature; I was twenty-two or twenty-three. I went to the pub – because, where I was training, there's the University of Ilorin, and there's a pub near there, so when I finished work, sometimes I'd go there just to relax before I went home.

One day, I saw this lady coming into the pub, and she

looked like the kind of... Well, she looked like Idayat, she looked like Chidinma! She looked like my kind of woman. I couldn't talk to her that day, but I regretted it, and for two months I was going to the pub just to see if she was going to come there. She didn't come for two good months, and I was about to give up, when one day I was at the pub and she came in.

I just stood up. I went up to talk to her, and I said, 'You were there on this day, you were wearing this...' and I told her what she was wearing and everything.

She said, 'Wow.'

So we exchanged greetings, and when she'd had a drink we walked out together, and after that we became friends. I didn't tell her what I felt towards her. We were just very close friends. Later on, after a couple of months, I noticed when we were walking, the way she'd look at girls... We began to talk more and got close, and I fell in love with her and we started a relationship. In Nigeria, two women are not allowed to hold hands. You go out as three or four. Two girls, or two boys, or two men together... it's full of meanings. The university is not far from where I worked, and she was doing tailoring training, so sometimes I would tell her to meet me at the university and we'd go to a restaurant and sit down, with some other people in between us, and we'd send signals and talk that way. I told my boss that I wanted a day off, and I didn't tell my parents I was going to take it off, so that I'd have more time to see her.

'She tried to protect me'

All through Azanat's story we see the contrast between the sweetness of new love and the violent hatred and abuse that was its punishment. This time, the violence extended to Azanat's mother.

One horrible day at home, all my half-brothers came and pounced on me and said, 'We know you are a lesbian, and this is an abomination.' And they were beating me. My mum came, she tried to protect me, but they were still doing it.

They said to her, 'You have an abomination child! She is not a right child!'

They beat us both so badly that my mum lost one of her legs. She had to have it amputated. I showed the Home Office pictures of her when she had two legs, and when she was amputated. She was in the hospital for a couple of months. The treatment was very expensive, so we had to sell the shop. And I was unable to see my girlfriend any more. My dad was abusing me and cursing me and saying, 'You're not a right child, you're an abomination child! We don't know where we were getting you from!' And all that.

They discharged my mother from the hospital, and when she came home, some of my friends' fathers told my father, 'Why don't you marry this girl out?' They said that my parents should marry me out and get some money for me. And they did.

The man that I was being married to, I didn't know him from anywhere, I'd only seen him once. He came to the hospital once when I was there, and gave my mum a lot of money. When she had come back to the house, that was the second time I was going to see him, for the introduction.

An abusive marriage

So they did the introduction for me, and they did a traditional wedding for me as well; and I got married. On my wedding day, I was not laughing, because this is somebody I don't even know, and he's really, really older than me: I'm talking about a sixty-six-year-old man. Yes! That's years older than me. The marriage was a Muslim thing, you know; they should marry me out.

So, I was not happy on that day, and he said, 'Do you want to talk to your mother?'

I said, 'Yes, I want to talk to my mother.'

And my mother said, 'I don't want to talk to you!'

And my father said, 'I don't want to talk to you!'

My husband already had two wives. I was the third one. When he wanted to sleep with me in the bedroom, I felt horrible. He said to me, 'You are a woman, why are you not enjoying it? There's no emotion in you!' He was always saying those things.

Then he told my mum that he wanted to take me abroad. I came with him to England. When we got to London, he said, 'Do you know, I've spent a lot of money on you, and I did not enjoy you as a wife. Now, here in England, I will make you pay for everything I've spent on you.'

I spent a week there before I ran away. He wanted to force me into prostitution; but it didn't happen, because I had eighty-four pounds with me, and I ran away from there.

Peace of mind

I came to Manchester. I had a friend from Nigeria here and she had said, when I got to Piccadilly I should ring her. I rang and rang until my phone died, and I had to find somewhere in Piccadilly to charge my phone. For three days I was ringing her. I didn't have anywhere to sleep for three nights; I was sleeping at the train station. I was walking about for three nights. It was December. It was winter; it was very cold.

On the third day, a woman came by, speaking my language on the phone. I went up to her and she was eager to talk to me. She said, 'Oh, what happened?' I told her I ran away from London and I didn't have anywhere to stay, because I was hoping to see a friend, I'd been calling her, and she was not picking up.

She said she was going to work now, but she would meet me again at six o'clock.

So before six o'clock that day I was already at the bus stop at Piccadilly, and at 6.05 she came. She was the first person who accommodated me. I just told her I'd run away from my husband; I didn't tell her about my sexuality. She was very good to me. I think she was a Christian. And that's when I first found peace of mind in England. She gave me a sofa in her house, and that's where I was till the Home Office assessed me.

'God loves us'

In Manchester, I found the Metropolitan Community Church. My third girlfriend, she was a Christian, and when I was telling her about my experience with Chidinma's grandparents, I told her, 'I don't like my religion. When my father is saying I should go and pray, I don't pray any more.'

And she said to me, 'This is what we are. God loves us. We didn't create ourselves, He created us. I didn't want to be like that, I tried to force my way out of it, but no, this is me.' But because of the society we belonged to, we couldn't say that out loud.

So, when I found out about the Metropolitan Community Church, I went there. And it was a woman there who told me about LISG. That was ten months ago.

LISG is my home, it's my family, it's one of the best things that ever happened to me in Manchester. That and the church, they are the best things that ever happened to me. LISG has supported me in so many ways – with finance, with social outings, all the friends I've made – and I've made firm relationships that will last many, many years. When I went for my interview at the Home Office and told them about LISG, the lady who interviewed me was impressed. I don't know if she knew about LISG already; I think she had to, because they gave me a supporting letter, and the church also gave me a letter. And the Home Office gave me my status, straight away!

I'm going to study. I want to do an advanced course, because I studied fashion design back home but in this country, you have to be a professional. I'd like to study nursing. Let me establish myself first; but in the future, I want to find my way into nursing.

At Manchester Pride last year, I was wearing this colourful thing, a rainbow, and a lady said to me, in my own language, 'You bloody lesbian, you deserve to die.' Because she was speaking in Yoruba, I felt everything that had happened to me in Nigeria come back. These are the people that kill you, in Nigeria. Everything bad that had happened to me in the past came back; I was traumatised. I almost committed suicide. I got help from the LGBT Foundation: from there I was re-referred to Think Ahead and to Manchester Rape Crisis, from that event.

'This is who I am'

What I would say to others is: accept who you are! Especially in this society, I can see such happy lesbians. Don't feel shy about who you are – we are a creation of God. There is nothing like 'abomination'. There is nothing like, 'No, it is wrong.' No. Accept who you are. I have accepted who I am. In the future, if I find someone I really love, I'm going to get married and put it on social media. It's going to be every-where. Yes! I'll tell them, in the UK I'm a lesbian, and I'm being accepted into society. So, why not?

In the future, if something happens to Nigeria and they change the law so it's going to favour LGBT people, I'll go there and tell them, 'I've been accepted in the UK, this is my life, this is who I am.' I'll be an activist for them. Because the killing is still going on there; the persecution is still going on, and they still have a law against gay people. They can't come out. It's getting worse. How long will somebody live in hiding? They have lesbians in Nigeria, but they live in hiding. Some of them are being forced into marriage, like I was, being forced not even to speak or anything.

So – accept yourself!

MARY

People who escape from horrific persecution in their own countries often make the journey to the UK on a visitor's visa. When these short-term visas run out, the holders become illegal immigrants. Their subsequent asylum process can then be made harder, because the Home Office will often assume that they came to the UK under false pretences. When they first arrive, they might also find that the 'sponsor' in the UK who helped them get the visa has withdrawn their support. This is what happened to Mary and her family when they fled from Kenya, and quite soon they became destitute. As with Azanat, the turning point in their story came with an act of kindness from a stranger. This time it was the generosity of a local shopkeeper, who helped them to understand and access the asylum system.

Mary grew up in a village in Kenya with her parents and paternal grandparents. She was a happy child until, in her early teens at a Catholic boarding school, she realised she was interested in girls. It was very painful for Mary to talk about the terrible things that happened to her and her family as a result of her being a lesbian – but she was absolutely determined to tell her story. As she says at the end, 'I always wished to get to this point, where I could talk about everything.'

My first crush was my teacher – obviously she was an adult, so I couldn't tell her at all. But I just came to realise that I was different, and that's when I realised for the first time that I had to keep it to myself. I was raised going to church all the time, and in church they would tell you that the way of God is a man marrying a woman, and that any other way is no good. So, it was really scary for me. As I was going along in my secondary school, just because I'm human, I would make friends with other girls. I remember that I opened up to a friend of mine. She was called Lana. She and I were so very close in friendship, we'd talk about so many things, and we were from the same village. I told her I'd got these feelings that were not in line with what everybody else would expect. I told her, 'If I were to get into a relationship, I would really want to have a girlfriend.' Lana was a bit older than me; I was fifteen and she was eighteen at that time. And when I opened up to her, to my surprise Lana was also a lesbian! It felt like heaven. It felt like, 'This is it! This is it, for me!' And because of how close we were, we started a relationship, in school.

It was dangerous. Lana was a prefect. It went on for a while, and I remember how we came to be caught. We used to have a small shop in the school. We called it the canteen, but it was a small shop: we used to sell biscuits and snacks to the students. The shop was run by some of the school clubs; Lana used to lead the debate club. And I remember in that week, when we got caught, it was her turn to have the key. So, on one Saturday evening, Lana and I locked ourselves inside the canteen. We used to have entertainments in the evenings – if some students wanted to have dancing, they could have music, and we could also have movies. So, we took advantage of that, and went to the canteen and locked ourselves up, and... I'd say, we started getting into it a little bit! While we were still inside, I remember hearing a knock on the door. We quickly dressed, and when we opened the door, it was the principal of the school. I think because we didn't switch off the lights of the canteen, and it was made of iron sheets, and when they're putting nails in the iron sheets, sometimes they leave tiny holes... I think the principal had been watching us, all along. So, when we opened the door, it was like, 'Now this is the end of our schooling!' She told us that she had been watching us, and she'd had tips from other students that me and Lana were doing something that was not right. Because she'd seen us, we couldn't start saying, 'No, it's not what you saw...'

It was at night, so she told us we were going to go to sleep, and tomorrow morning she was going to call in our parents. It was so embarrassing! First of all, my parents were really shocked, and they played a blame game. My mum would say it was because I was hanging out with Lana, she was a bad influence; and Lana's mother would say it was me. We tried to tell our parents, 'It's not like I'm a bad influence, or she's a bad influence, it's just us, you know?'

The principal said, 'You can't stay in this school any more.' But my parents really spoke with her, and they made me promise that I would never, ever do such a thing again. So, I wrote a letter to apologise, and to say that I would never do that again. I was not suspended from the school, and Lana was not suspended either. So, we stayed. I wouldn't say we stopped being together; we just didn't get caught any other time!

'Devil-worshippers'

Things were about to get worse for the girls. As the news spread through the school and then through their home village, they were ostracised. Other parents even claimed that Mary and Lana's parents must be devil-worshippers if they had lesbian daughters and allowed the girls to stay in the family. This was in 2006. The following year, a sad loss for Mary's family was used as further evidence against them.

My grandmother, my father's mother, passed on. She had had a stroke on one side of the body, and she used to just like to get out of the house to get some sunshine, and sit down. I remember she was just sitting there, when she passed on. That's when the pressure became acute, with my mum and dad being accused of being devil-worshippers, and the whole village saying that they had sacrificed her. It was a very bad situation for us, and there was pressure on my parents to send me away. But they couldn't just throw me out of the house. So, then they started putting pressure on my mum and dad that I needed to be circumcised, to cleanse me of evil. My mother would not – she told me she couldn't put me through that – and they refused to do it. But I think the pressure kept getting worse. Then in 2008, a year later, my grandfather died. It was just a heart attack; he just fell and died. And so that increased the pressure. Like, now they had sacrificed the two parents!

People in my country do believe these things. For instance, my dad sold some land, so he had some money. But the moment that you start having money, they don't even consider what you've done, it's like you're getting it from somewhere occult, and the money is not real. They have this mentality that if you touch that money, you might die, or have bad things happen in your family. At that point when my grandfather and my grandmother died, and because my parents had never let me go through circumcision, it seemed the only reason they would support me must be because they were devil-worshippers. So, after the funeral of my grandfather, my dad decided we needed to sell the place and move.

On the move

They sold the land that we were living on, and we moved to a place in the northern part of Kenya. We'd lived in the central part, so it's a big long journey. We started life there: at first we rented a house, and then my dad got a job and we found a house to live in, and my sister – she was small, back then – settled into primary school. It was still a village, where we were living. I come from a tribe called Kikuyu; it's a very large tribe in Kenya, and scattered over many areas. So, after we moved, three months in, someone from my community spotted us. There is still a big number of Kikuyu in Malaba, and someone spotted us who knew our family. I remember how the problems started for us there. My mum was in church and the preacher told her to stand up in front of everybody. And he told the whole church that her daughter was a lesbian, and we'd been sent away from the place we were living in Mukuka, and we'd come to Malaba to recruit more girls to be lesbians. I wasn't there, but he told everyone that I, her daughter, would recruit more girls; and they must not trust us, because we were devil-worshippers. So, from that day, we were not allowed to go to that church any more. My mother had to leave the church. It was so embarrassing. So now the news started spreading, and even when we shopped, if we went to the shop and wanted to give the shopkeeper our money, they wouldn't take it, because they thought it was not real money. They thought it was devil-worshippers' money, money from a lesbian family.

It became so bad, it started affecting my little sister in school, because other kids would ask her to explain to them what I do as a lesbian! She was just a small child back then, and sometimes she would say, 'I don't want to go to school.' Because of that thing of me being known as a lesbian, the teachers would not support her. Even though they knew that she was being harassed by other children in school, they would not support her. It got so she had to stop going to school. And it got so that it was difficult for us to stay in Malaba. We'd moved there in 2009, and we lived there up to the end of 2010. We moved again, to Mombasa. So now we'd moved from the north all the way to the south of Kenya. My dad had sold our land in Malaba, so we rented a small house, and after a time, he was able to build a little house for us, a little family house. My mum used to sell clothes, not expensive ones, just everyday clothes, and my dad used to do taxi jobs. We had a car, and he was able to get a little cash and bought another car. When he bought a car, he would buy it at a cheaper price and sell it at a higher price, and that kept us going. When we moved to Mombasa, it was 2011. I got a job as a waitress in a hotel, and my sister also got a school to attend.

Trizah

In Mombasa, I met another lady. She was called Trizah. I met her in the hotel where I used to work. She was a client there; and I'd say she was one of the respected clients of the hotel, a customer the hotel would not want to lose. She was a Kenyan lady. I got to know her, and she was a lesbian as well. We started a relationship. We would always meet at her house; sometimes we'd talk at the hotel, when she came. I remember one evening I was seated at home, and I received a message on my phone, from my workplace. In Kenya, we have this way of sending money through the phone, it's called M-Pesa. So I received a message saying I'd received some money, and the message that followed said my services were no longer required at the workplace, because they'd found out I had been having a lesbian relationship with their client, Trizah, and that is not the sort of behaviour they want at the workplace. They explained that it's a risk for the hotel if I continue working there, because if the community found out they might burn down the hotel. They would not let me back there any more.

When I received the message, I forwarded it to Trizah and asked her what she thought about it. She told me not to worry, I could always find another job. So, we agreed that I would see her the following day. But, to my surprise, when I went to Trizah's house, she was gone! There was nothing in the house. Her phone was off. I don't know, but I think she was scared as well, because Mombasa is a Muslim city, and that is something they would never support. I think she was really afraid. Trizah was a Christian, but Mombasa is hugely dominated by Muslims.

So, Trizah was gone, and I went home and told my mother about the message I'd received. To be honest, I hadn't told her about my relationship with Trizah, but at that point I told her I'd been fired because of having a relationship, and she was like, 'Okay, we'll just find another job.' My mum is a wonderful woman. She started getting threats from people, at her business. So now they knew who I was; and the story – that my grandparents died because of it – always followed us everywhere. Even when my mum was in Mombasa, she'd get threats like, 'Oh, we know you sacrificed your parents.

We will not let you sacrifice anybody here. We will not let you have your lesbian daughter in this community!'

So, nobody would buy her clothes; and my dad, when he was doing the taxi business, nobody would want to be involved with him. It seemed like we must all suffer, because it followed my sister in school also. The thing that used to annoy me was that not even the teachers would stand up for her, because they also didn't want her in the school. It was really hard for her. And even the shopkeeper close to us would not take our money. We'd travel very far to go and buy things; and at times we would still find that people there knew us. So, if we got lucky, and somebody wanted to sell something to us, we would say, 'It's our good day!'

'In broad daylight'

Once again, their lives were unbearable, so Mary's parents sold all they had, at a loss, to move across the country for the third time. In 2014, the family settled into a small house which Mary's father built for them on cheap land in a village near Nairobi. Mary took a job as a waitress in the city. Sadly, this would turn out to be not just a move for the worse, but a move into lethal danger.

Whilst I was working in Nairobi, I got to know a lady; she was a cashier in a hotel. I got to know her, we got to be close, and at some point, I shared what I'd been through with her. She was bisexual, which also was not right in their society. We never had a relationship, but we were close friends. Then, unfortunately for her, she was killed. She was at the bus stop, and all these men came to harass her because she was wearing a short skirt, and they started undressing her, and they pulled her skirt, and stamped on her. It was in broad daylight, but no police came to help her. She passed on, because by the time someone took her to hospital, they had really harassed her, and she didn't make it.

Before that, my father had been asked to go and see the village elders, and he had been told that he either needed to get me out of that place, or he needed to circumcise me. My father said he couldn't do that to me. They knew he couldn't send me away; there was nowhere for me to go. My mum had been attending a Presbyterian church in Kikuyu, and they knew about us, too. So, what happened next, I think the whole community had organised it.

A night of horror

One night, when we were asleep, I remember the grilles on the windows being cut. Our house was made of iron sheets, and the windows in Kenya are not like they are here, usually there are grilles inside. They did it really fast, so by the time I woke up in my room I could see torches and flashing lights inside the house and I was scared, because I thought, 'What's going on?' There were five men who came inside, and I didn't even have the opportunity to hide, or to do anything. Someone dragged my blankets off my bed. There were three men in my room, and one was grabbing me and holding me, and they were all saying the same thing: 'Have you come here to recruit more girls to be lesbians like you are?' They were saying horrible things, like I'd allowed my mind to be brainwashed by western things (because they believe being lesbian is something from the west). And I couldn't even speak, I was so terrified, so scared. I've never been so scared.

My room was opposite my sister's room, and at the end was my mum and dad's room, and at the front was the living room. Some of the men went in to my parents. I could hear they were beating my mum and dad in their room, and another one was beating my sister. Right now, she has a big body, but back then she was really small. While they were asking me those questions, asking me and beating me at the same time (I still have the scars on my legs), I remember one of them saying that they were going to teach me a lesson. And the lesson was horrible, because they raped me. All three of them that were in my room. That's when I got pregnant with my child.

After that incident, I had to go to hospital; I spent a few days in hospital. And when I came back, the church sent some leaders to speak to me. All they could tell me was that God had put a life inside me, and abortion is illegal in Kikuyu anyway, so they couldn't tell me to do an abortion; all they could tell me was that I had no right to take away that life. My father didn't support abortion either. So, I decided to keep the child, because when I looked at the options, even if I decided to do an abortion it would have to be backstreet, and would have its risks. And my father and my mum were supportive and said they would help me raise the child.

So, after that incident, in 2015, I gave birth to my daughter. And we carried on with life. I felt I was very stigmatised because I was a single mother and had no idea who the father of my child was, and I wasn't working, because I had lost the job I was doing as a waitress. It was very difficult for me. Sometimes I couldn't even leave our home, because if I went out of doors, everyone would be looking at me and pointing at me, and I could always feel it. It just made me feel terrible about myself, and if I stayed inside the house, I felt safe and I felt at peace.

So, we did carry on with life, but still there was that problem of people not accepting our money, and having to travel far to buy things; and, by this time, we were not financially good at all. People were still putting much pressure on my father about how he should get me married or, if not, he should circumcise me. My mum's parents, who were well-respected elders of the community, were supporting the idea of me getting circumcised. Even my mum's brother and sister would not talk to her; none of them wanted anything at all to do with us. So, even if you ask my sister right now, she says she has no cousins, because none of them have ever been close to her, none of them have ever wanted anything to do with her.

A second attack

In 2016, there was another incident. When the first one happened, in 2014, we did report it to the police, but they said, 'This is a safe village, nothing like that has ever happened.' They said they were going to investigate, but nothing ever came of it. In 2016, another incident happened, and it was almost the same as the first one. They came and started cutting out the grilles, and this time they were saying, 'Everybody has to die in this home!' This time they came in and took all of us out of our bedrooms to the living room, and I'm telling you they really, really hit us and stabbed us, like this time they really wanted to end things. They raped me in my mouth, in the living room, and they were beating my dad, beating and beating him...

How we got away was like this. My sister, who was sixteen at that time, had been tied by the hands, and they were telling her to watch what happens to people who do not want to live like humans. At that time my child was one year old; they had put her on top of the table and they had started undressing her. I don't know what intentions they had, but they had started undressing her. My sister, because she had been tied up, they were not putting eyes on her so much, and they were starting with my dad, my mum and me. She really struggled, and got her hands out, and she grabbed my daughter and ran. After the first incident, we had installed an alarm in the house, near to the bathroom; she went in and pressed it, and when it started ringing it was really loud. So, these men started scattering and running away. We could hear them jumping on the walls and running.

When they had left, I got out and went to my neighbours' house and asked if they could help us. At first, they were looking through the window, saying, 'Who is this?' I was telling them, 'Please, please, help us!' And I remember the neighbour opened the door, pulled me in and closed the door, because he was not sure if they were still around. I quickly told him that they had beaten my dad and he needed to be taken to the hospital; also my mum had been beaten, they had really cut her. So, he took my dad to the hospital. But first of all, we had to go through the police station, and the police had to write a report that they had seen my dad, and only then they took him to hospital. Then the neighbour's wife took me and my mum to the hospital. Sadly, my dad didn't make it. He'd lost too much blood. When he got to the hospital the doctors said, 'He's not alive.' Me and my mum had to stay in hospital for longer, because I couldn't even walk, my left leg was badly cut in the same place they had been cutting me the last time; the same place. So, we stayed in hospital for five days, and after we came out of hospital, we buried my dad. It was a small funeral, really.

At the police station

A month after this brutal attack and the death of her father, Mary was told to report for further questioning at the police station. She was shocked to find herself under arrest: the police were claiming she knew who had killed her father. But that was only a pretext for torturing her.

I stayed in the police station for three days. I had been put by myself, what they called solitary, on my own. When I was inside there, I would be told to stand up from six o'clock till ten o'clock. They kept telling me that I'm going to rot in hell for my lesbianism. That is what they told me. I would be given one meal a day; it was just pushed under the door. After I had left hospital, my leg was still hurting, and I was being told to stand from six to ten. After that, they would let me sit till the following day. They would just say, 'Sit! Stand up!' And they would call me all sorts of names, and nobody was allowed to come and see me.

My mum was always a church woman, and she knew a priest, who came and paid – he bribed the police – to let me out of there. That's the way it works in Kenya. When I got out of the cell, we didn't go back to the house; we went to Dakuru, where that priest lived. Everything was really scary, because we had just lost my dad, and now we had to move; but, after all that, we couldn't go back to that house. It was too scary. So, we went and lived in the church compound in Dakuru and we changed our dress: we used to dress like Muslims, so people wouldn't realise it was us. Three days after we moved, our house – the house where everything happened – was burned down.

That was when the priest said that he could organise for us to get visas to leave the country; maybe we would come back after everything had settled down. I thought it was a good idea, but it was scary as well. All this time, even with everything that had happened, even when we had to keep moving, I always felt safe, because my dad would say, 'Ah, don't worry.' But when he was gone, it felt like a house without a roof: we were not covered at all, we felt like we were lost. And I realised, there's nobody to tell me not to worry any more, because my dad always told me, 'Don't worry.' He would always find a solution, like, 'We've got to move!' and we would move. And now he was no longer here, and I felt that it was my fault, because I felt like he had died defending me. After my dad passed, during those days before we got the visas to leave, I and my family got so depressed, and my mum lost so much weight.

Escape

In Dakuru, the priest arranged the first visa. They agreed this was to go to their mother, but the thought of being separated from her was too much for Mary's sister, who made a suicide attempt. Some time later, their mother did travel to the UK on a visitor's visa.

We had visitors' visas, because the priest had someone he knew over here, who had given the invitation. The only problem was that when my mum arrived here, that person refused to pick her up, so she got stranded. She was in

Leicester. This person refused to pick her up, but she told her that she could organise a place for her to stay, so my mum had to go and live in a place called Slough. That person said she was afraid some stories might get back to our country, but that she was supporting us, and if my mum had any problem, she could always talk to her. She refused to pick her up, though. It was the same for us – she gave us the invitation, and we came, and she had promised she was going to pick us up at the airport. We arrived at eight o'clock and we called her till 2pm and she did not answer. My mum had to come all the way to pick us up; we had arrived at Birmingham, and she had to come all the way from Slough. I remember, that evening, the lady sent us a message saying that she was afraid, she'd been hearing stories from Kenya that if she associated with us, her family back in Kenya was going to get in danger. So she told us that she didn't want any more communication with us.

The kind shopkeeper

Two months later, they heard that the priest who had helped them (and had sent them money) had been killed, leaving them stranded. They had nothing to live on. They were obtaining food on credit from a local shop.

The shopkeeper said, 'You should go and seek asylum.'

The only understanding I had of an asylum was to do with mental issues, a mental hospital! So I said, 'What is asylum?'

He told me, 'If you know you can't go back to your country, you tell the government what you have been through, and they can give you protection from your country.'

So, first of all, it was scary for me, because I didn't know how the government here works, and the understanding I had about the government in my country was horrible. I went back to my house and told my mum what the shopkeeper was telling me, and at first we said, 'No way!'

Then I told my mum, 'Maybe you can go and speak to him, and you'll be able to understand more.' But my mum's English is not so good, so I went there with her, and told the man to explain to us again about what asylum is, and whether we would get arrested, and all that.

He said, 'No, you won't get arrested. Get a train from Slough and go to London, go to Croydon and just go and tell them what is wrong with you, and your fear, that you don't want to go back to your country.'

We were really struggling. The shopkeeper had told us, 'If you don't even have a house and you are struggling, they might help you, they might give you a house.'

We went back to the house and looked at it, and we thought we should try it. But we didn't know about how we should do it.

Struggles with the Home Office

The shopkeeper knew other people seeking asylum; he gave the family the address for the Home Office in Croydon, along with the money to travel there.

When we went to Croydon, the mistake we made was, we hadn't booked an appointment. When we got there, the lady at the front desk said, 'You need an appointment! We can't see you today.'

And that day we had taken our bags and everything.

She told us, 'You need to call this number for an appointment, and come back another day.'

So we had to go back home. We went back to Slough.

Mary's screening interview, when it was finally arranged, was a week before her mother's. The interview was not easy.

They said I had lied at the airport, that I had a visitor's visa when I was really coming to seek asylum. So I had to explain the whole thing: that I didn't know anything about seeking asylum. They took me through the screening interview questions, and I answered them. It was a struggle also to get them to give me accommodation, because they were thinking that I need to go back and wait for my mum's interview, so we could come back together. The first person who interviewed me had refused to give me accommodation, but, by God's grace, he transferred me to another person, and the next person was good, he agreed. I had to stay in the hostel and wait for my family, who came the following week. I remember the first night I was given the accommodation: the bed was so good! It was like in a hotel. I slept for ages!

Their screening interview took the whole day, and they were also given accommodation, so that was really good. My mum said, 'It's different, the government is really different.' Not like the way you would expect the police in Kenya to treat you. It's different here. I always say that the people here in the UK are really good, and welcoming. Not the same as my country! I do have friends who tell me that sometimes they get into a bus, and nobody wants to sit next to them... but I would say, for me, I've never experienced that. Usually for me, the people here are generally good.

After we did the screening interviews and stayed in the hotel, they moved us to Liverpool. And from Liverpool they brought us down to Manchester. While we were living in Manchester, we went for our main interview, in 2018. They had linked my case and my mum's together, so we went for the interview on the same day, but in different rooms. After we made the claim, they rejected it, so my solicitor said, 'We need to appeal.' She said the reason they gave was rubbish. I had submitted two hospital reports that they had given me back in Kenya, and the Home Office said they had been written by the same person, and with the same pen! They said the handwriting looks the same in the two reports for 2014 and 2016. But when you look at the documents, it's clear that the handwritings are very different.

When I appealed and went to court, the judge listened

to my case and agreed about my sexuality. He also looked at the claim that the handwriting looks the same – and told the Home Office they should have taken those documents back to my country to be checked. The judge said he did agree that I am at risk if I go back to my country, but he thought my mum and my sister would be safe! So, the reason he gave for not accepting my appeal was that if I go back with them, they should be able to protect me.

My solicitor looked at that and was like, 'Not on the evidence so far!' But by the time we got the decision letter from the judge, the days had got too much, we couldn't appeal any more, and my solicitor said we need to put in a fresh claim. At the moment she is preparing our statements, and we're looking forward to seeing what she's going to prepare, this weekend, and we're going to submit it at Liverpool.

My mum was given therapy, too, and she's been for counselling. It's in English, though her first language is Kikuyu and her English is not so good: you need to speak slowly for her to understand. She has a friend that comes to teach her English at home. She's working hard on it. My daughter is at school, she's in reception, and my sister got a place at college. Myself, I started volunteering with Refugee Action in Manchester. Usually I'm at the front desk, receiving the people who are coming in.

'A human like any other'

And how did I come to LISG? Let me start from the beginning...

First of all, my solicitor gave me a list of contacts at the LGBT Foundation in Manchester. But I'd never attended therapy, never been to counselling; I had that stigma still in my head, I was afraid of telling anyone else what I am. Because it was a new country, I was really afraid.

Even after everything I went through in my country, I

never got any mental health support. I think mental health issues are not a priority in my country. I always just kept everything that happened, inside me. And when I came here, and I had to tell it to the Home Office, that's when I realised that things are really heavy, inside of you. But when I started going for counselling, it did help me to realise that it's not my fault. What happened was not my fault.

I used to lock myself in the house a lot. I never used to go out. When I came to this country, I was small; but, because I stayed in the house, I kept eating and eating and I got so big! When I started to go for counselling, it made me realise that I need to come out and mix with people who are like me. So, I got up the courage to come and look for this LGBT Foundation, and they gave me a list of groups, and the first group I joined was called Women of Colour. I used to come every month, and that's when I found out about LISG.

They were so kind. When they replied, they sounded polite and good. My email was responded to by Karen and she said that she would like to meet me before she could introduce me to the group. And I came and met her and two other ladies. They received me so well, they were really listening, they didn't judge me, and I just felt like, 'Wow! This is what I'd been looking for!' I felt like it was home for me.

They did welcome me, and they invited me to an end of year party that was happening in December. When I went there, I felt like all those days I'd been locking myself in the house, I'd been missing out, a lot! Because I found people who are like-minded, people who are so polite and accepting, and not judging; good people. I would say LISG has really empowered me. The way I used to feel down, the way I used to feel afraid – it's not the same any more. I feel like I'm a person like any other person, and I'm human like any other human. I've met brilliant women in LISG, women who've also fought their own battles in their own way, and it's like home for me. It's an empowering group. And I think that meeting a group like LISG, and also going for counselling, has enabled me to speak the way I speak now – otherwise I'd still be locking myself in the house.

I used to feel like if I went out, there was somebody watching me; but now, I've really come to be myself. I always wished to get to this point, where I could talk about everything.

~

Mary is still awaiting the outcome of her fresh claim.

SAM & JERRY

I hadn't met Sam before our interview, but she had offered to contribute to the book, so we arranged to meet at the offices of the LGBT Foundation in central Manchester. It was a convenient time, Sam said, because she and her partner would already be in town that day to attend their college classes. It wasn't until they both appeared, however, that I realised I had two interviewees, not one! Sometimes, when I sit down with a couple to do a life history interview, I end up with two separate stories; but sometimes, as with Sam and Jerry, it is impossible to tease their narratives apart. So here they are, in dialogue. As with many of the contributors, their names have been changed and some distinguishing details left out, for their safety.

We are all familiar with the romantic story of two young people in love, running away from their families to be together; but that story rarely tells of the struggles they face afterwards. When Sam and Jerry arrived in the UK, with the dream of making a new life together, they did not realise that the worst was yet to come. Their journey to refugee status was to take a heavy toll on their mental health, and – as with Mary and her family – a large part of their suffering was having to watch each other's pain. Both experienced periods of serious depression. Sam felt she had lost everything: not just a comfortable, privileged life and the celebrity status her sporting prowess had given her in Pakistan, but also her role as Jerry's mentor and protector. Jerry, struggling in a strange language and an alien culture, fought to maintain her own sanity and to pursue their asylum claim, while she watched Sam sink deeper and deeper into despair.

So this is not just the story of two people on a journey: it is the story of a relationship that has been tested to its limits by adversity and has survived. Sometimes, as LGBTQ+ people are so fond of saying, 'love wins'.

Sam: I was born in 1985 in a small city in a rural part of Pakistan, near to the village of my ancestors. I have three sisters and a brother. When I was a teenager, my parents shifted to the city of Gujrat: that's where I did my A levels and went to university. I am from a Muslim family. We are very religious, very strict, especially my mum: she wears the *hijab* and *burka*. That was not an obligation for me – as a child, I even used to wear jeans. They never stopped me, and there was not a restriction on going out or studying; but there were other restrictions, like marriage and choosing partners. It was very conservative. When I was sixteen or seventeen and at high school, my family wanted me to marry and things like that – and I was not accepting those things. That was one of the turning points of my life, because I suffered from depression for a year.

But then, slowly, I started focussing on my studies and education and I was fine again. Things changed because I was very good at sport and wanted to make it my career. I was lucky that when I went to university I got the chance to play for a team. It was hard initially for my family to allow me to do that, but then they did. I was nearly twenty-one when I started playing. I got selected and started going out with the team. When I started playing, permission was one of the big problems. For two years, I wore a headscarf. I got to the stage where I didn't want to wear it any more. It took a long time to get my parents' permission, but then I took off the scarf. Although I stopped wearing a *hijab,* my beliefs hadn't changed; it was just not suitable for playing in. I went on playing and I became part of the national team.

I was still single then. I had met Jerry but at first we were only friends. She was a junior player and she asked me to teach her. In 2010 she came to visit Gujrat and, that same year, I got picked for Pakistan.

Jerry: [laughing] I was lucky for her!

Sam: By the end of 2011, you can say we were in a good relationship. We were close. We had known each other around one and a half years, we were good friends, and I was her teacher as well.

'Girls were really impressed'

Jerry: She had another girlfriend before me. She was a little flirty!

Sam: Yes, actually I used to like somebody, but it was just teasing – it wasn't a physical thing. But yes, I liked girls. It started when I was sixteen or seventeen; I didn't know why I liked girls. When I was in second year Intermediate, that was the first time I started liking a girl.

Jerry: So, before our relationship, there was one girl. But she was a horrible girl.

Sam: It was not a relationship! Basically, it was a beginning for me. I was like, okay, we are friends. I had no idea what an intimate relationship was. I did like her...

Jerry: [teasing] She was horrible!

Sam: And I used to tell her, 'Look, I feel like I want to kiss you,' but I did not know... There was something stopping me. Maybe I didn't know how to do things. Believe me, Jerry was the first one. We took so long to get close to each other – so slowly we learned! It took lots of time.

Jerry: This other girl was in her regional team.

Sam: But it was not, like, a close relationship. It was the way Jerry is saying – flirting!

Jerry Yes, she was a little flirty, I know! But that girl... They had a connection. They would eat together, go home together...

Sam: I am not praising myself, but I was a very good player and those girls, they got attracted to me. They were like, really impressed. And my family are highly rated people. So, they wanted to be friends. They wanted me to like them, and wanted to be my friend. I was fine with it, but they were not my type of girls. Good for friendship, but if they start loving me another way, it's not my fault! Then they started picking me up, dropping me off and slowly they started coming to my house. I was going to their houses, spending nights there, and they were giving me too many expensive gifts. And I was like, 'Okay, they are friends.'

So when that girl showed her intention after a year or so, I said, 'Look, I like you but...' I didn't like her like that. If Jerry had not come into my life, then, maybe... Perhaps she knew something about what happens between girls; she was expecting something from me. She was very flirty and maybe she thought she could start something. But I didn't. Eventually Jerry came into my life, and that girl became her biggest enemy!

A traditional upbringing

Jerry's upbringing, in a small village, had been less privileged and more strictly traditional than Sam's.

Jerry: I was born into a Pashtun family. My dad, my mum and my brothers were very strict in their religion but, when I was a child, I used to go outside with my father and my brothers. If my brothers were playing, whatever they were doing, I would go with them. I don't remember playing with the girls. School was co-educational from nursery to eighth class, and during break I used to play with the boys: team games and all these things. Now, we were living in a small village and the people there were typical village people; they didn't like a girl to play with boys. They don't want to see girls outside. But from childhood it was like this for me: I didn't like to play with girls. If the boys went swimming somewhere, I was with them. I played games a lot. And the neighbours were always telling my father, 'Stop your daughter playing with boys! This is not good!'

So, after that, slowly it changed. After school I used to go to *madrasa* for religious study, and on Saturday some computer classes, and then at home studying; and our father did not allow me to go outside. But when my family were asleep in the afternoons, or at night-time when he was working far away, I would get out. Then the neighbours started again, saying, 'Oh your daughter is again playing with boys. This is not good. This is shame!' And then my father started beating me and saying, 'Why are you doing this?' I was very young – about seven.

It was in school that I first started liking girls. My science teacher, she was nice to me, I don't know why. Maybe she understood, maybe she loved me, but I feel it was from then that I liked girls more than boys. It was only a feeling. I didn't know about what girls do together.

We were living in a small village and even my parents were not allowed to watch TV. So, it was very strict for us.

When I was fourteen, my father forced me into an engagement with someone I didn't know. I was in computer class one day and my sisters came to my institute and said, 'Let's go to the beauty salon, you have your engagement party today!'

I said, 'What?' I was shocked. It was the first I knew about it.

So, I was engaged at just fourteen. After that things got worse for me and I was always fighting with my father. Then, after three years, I was married.

Sam: At seventeen, she got married to that man!

'Treated like an animal'

Jerry: That man and his family were living in Afghanistan. We didn't know that before. And he was very aged. Much older than me. Even before the marriage, he would beat me and tell me, 'Don't go for study, don't do this...'

Sam: She got married, she went to Afghanistan, and that man was not good to her. He did not allow her even to see her father and brothers. They would go there and he would say, 'She's not here,' and wouldn't let her see them.

Jerry: No, they were not good. My father had not found out any information about them. You have to know about someone if you're giving your daughter to them! But for him it was all about respect: if I broke my marriage, what would people think of my family? So, I had no contact with my father or any of my family. I was losing my mind, because I was all day in one room. You weren't allowed to go outside whenever you liked. They were treating me like an animal. There were six brothers and five sisters. His mother was the worst woman!

Sam: It was such a huge house, and they asked her to work alone there, to clean and to cook food for all those people.

Jerry: I was only seventeen. So, then I thought, if my father can't do anything, I don't have a phone, I don't have any contact with anyone and they don't allow me to do anything, let's finish everything. I tried suicide. I took twenty pills, and I just looked at this guy and said, 'It's because of you.' If you read the Quran, if the girl doesn't want to marry, you can't force her. In our religion it says this, so how is it they were doing this with me? Even after that they didn't take me to hospital; I don't know how I'm still alive.

When I woke up, my brother was there. No one had informed him, it was just that my father was worried and had said, 'Go there and ask if your sister is fine or not.' So, when he came, I was not fine. Then the fighting started and my father came. I had totally lost my mind. I didn't recognise him: I forgot his name, everything.

We went to court – the police were involved – and my father brought me back to Pakistan. It was UNICEF who helped me: a kind of organisation that saves women. I think my brother went to a police station and they called them, and then everything was step by step. I don't remember everything. I do remember that I went in front of the judge three times and he was very angry with those people. He said, 'She's a child! Why are you doing these things?'

They tried to blame it all on me: 'She stole our gold and she was running away and we caught her.'

The judge was angry with the mother. He said, 'Don't lie!' And he said, 'She's a child. We checked everything: she doesn't have anything of yours and she's not in her senses. What did you do to her, this girl?'

And after that we didn't see them. But when we went back to Pakistan, they contacted the Taliban, they gave some money to those bad people, and every day men were calling and threatening my father: 'We will do this to you... We will put a bomb in your father's car, or your son's car.'

One day, I was just so angry, I took the phone and I said, 'Come! Come to our house! If you want to talk with me, I am that girl. Come!'

So he came to my house and I was very angry. He was sitting in front of me and I said, 'Are you Muslim?'

He said, 'Yes.'

'If you are Muslim, why are you doing this? Why are you giving us threats?' I told the whole story. 'Is that in your Islam? Your Islam is giving you this permission? Why are you people doing this?'

Then after that he was quiet. My brother and father were quiet and were looking at me quite shocked, saying, 'Why is she speaking?'

I said, 'I have been to *madrasa* and I have read the Quran. I am not uneducated. I know everything about Islam, and you don't need to do anything like this.'

So after that he was lost, that person!

And then my father realised he wasn't real Taliban, because real Taliban is not like this. Fake Taliban, you could say.

Afterwards, I told my father, 'Listen, now. This is my life, don't force me to do anything. This is my second life, and I will make my life my own.' I started a job in an NGO, and started to play squash.

First meeting

Jerry was ready to make up for lost time and for the childhood where her love of games had been so deplored. She was working on her squash game with a top coach when she was invited to try out for another sport – one she had only watched on television! It was a fantastic opportunity. She travelled to the match with high expectations...

Sam: I was a senior player by then, and they wanted me to go to Charsadda and meet new players and play a match there. Then I met her and she was very good. She was all the time laughing, laughing, and coming and teasing me, and I just treated her like a little kid: 'You want to have ice cream? You want to have an ice lolly?' I bought an ice lolly and gave it to her!

Jerry: Because I wanted her to know I was enjoying my life! I was starting my new life, and I wanted to forget the past.

Sam: At that time, I had no intention of making friends with her. One of the senior players from the Peshawar team told me her story and said maybe she was a troubled person, so I should stay away. She was explaining Jerry's situation.

Jerry: [teasing] Actually she was trying to flirt with her.

Sam: C'mon!

Jerry: Yeah, I know her!

Sam: [smiling] Anyone who meets or greets me, she thinks they are flirting with me!

Jerry: Sam had come from another city to play our team, and it's our culture to give respect to guests, so I was happy to see her. It was very exciting for me, playing a good game against such a senior player.

That first meeting was full of teasing and joshing. Jerry played well and was delighted to find she had impressed Sam.

Jerry: And then she said, 'Come to Gujrat. You have a talent.' In Peshawar, where I lived, we don't have the facility for women – still we don't have it – so she said, 'Come to Gujrat and start training with me at my club.'

First of all, I had to find a job there. It was very difficult to convince my family to let me go. Also, when I was on that tour, I had told my family I was at a workshop for my NGO. But my brother saw my picture in the newspaper. His friend, our neighbour, showed it to him and said, 'Is that your sister?'

My brother said, 'No.' But he brought it home. A picture of me, holding a trophy, with my team! So, when I came back, he said, 'You were at a workshop, yeah? This is your workshop?'

The whole story came out. My father was very angry.

So I had to look for a job in Gujrat, because I knew it would be very difficult for me to go there otherwise. Every day I was fighting with my brother and father, but now, this is my life: I will live the way I like. I found a job in an NGO I enjoyed. I started living in a hostel and Sam was supporting me a little bit, because I was very new in that city. And from that day, we – well, she will tell you.

Working together

Sam: At that first match she told me, 'I want to go on playing,' so when she came to Gujrat, I asked if she wanted me to train her. After six months, I got selected into the national team and by that time she was learning from me. So that was the part where we started getting more, you know... like, good friends.

Jerry: Then we started working hard together, supporting each other.

Sam: When I got selected for the team, she was also playing very well. Everyone was saying, 'Oh, she got good training from Sam.' Then, in 2012, we decided we would get an apartment. I said, 'You can stay there. Sometimes I can come – my family is sometimes away and I can come and stay with you.' So we started living together, because obviously by that time we were in a relationship. We didn't want to show it to anybody, because we were at a prestige level of sport; that was also a factor. So then we had an apartment. It was like our first home.

But we were terribly shocked when a girl started following us all the time, and spreading the news everywhere.

Jerry: 'Look,' and, 'Something is happening with your friend. They are not with boys, they are training and living together…'

'Then it got worse'

Sam: They were asking me, these girls, 'We play with you, give *us* coaching.' They were pushing me. 'You are *our* friend. Stop focussing on *her*, she is from another region! Why are you not giving your own team members training?'

So they were doing conspiracies all the time. They even came and tried to attack Jerry in the stadium. They even damaged my car. Yeah, these girls did this! They spread rumours all over the city during the national tournament: 'Sam is taking bribes from girls. She is taking money and training them, having favourites and putting them in the team.'

At that time, I was out of the team, so how was I putting girls in the team? And taking money from them? That time was very stressful, and we were afraid they might do anything.

Jerry: Then people started to harass me. We were at the ground from morning to night. We were very hard working and wanted to do something with our lives. But that girl did this shit and after that, the boys started laughing at us.

Some of them started telling me, 'I want to be friends with you,' and when I ignored them, they said, 'Oh, you and Sam have a relationship!' It was a shit thing. It felt as if everyone was looking our way. If I have something with her, it's my personal matter, not yours! We tried hard to keep it secret.

Sam: Over there, it's not like anybody gets an exact idea what a person's life is like. But those girls were thinking, 'They must have something between them.' And it can spread. Even my family were asking, 'Why do you spend nights there? It's not good.'

Then people were trying to inform my family: 'Look, your girl is not in good hands.' It was very stressful for me.

Jerry was in Gujrat in our apartment, and my parents were saying, 'No, you cannot go there now. Choose one day or two days.'

I was saying, 'No, I cannot do that any more. I want to stay there.'

Then it was like, 'Okay, three or four days.'

Sometimes it was very hard. But when they went to work outside the city, it was easier for me to spend time there.

Jerry: Then her servant told her family, 'They have something going on.'

Sam: Yes. They had given me a guard, a boy who used to take care of my things – my car and keys and things like that – because Pakistan is not safe for a woman alone, so it's good if you have a man with you when you are travelling.

He told my family, 'There is something between them. I think so.'

So they started taking more notice, and took it into their minds that something was going on. It was getting worse for both of us.

Jerry: Then my family started. 'Why are you are spending so much time in Gujrat? You have no job, you are only playing sport there.'

Sam: She hadn't told them she had a job, or that I was supporting her. So we were hiding things from them. And it was getting worse for us day by day. We had changed apartments three times, but those girls were still chasing us.

I was coming to the UK with the team, and I said to Jerry, 'Why don't we both go?' I was trying to think what I could do to help us. I said, 'Instead of my going there and being without you for so long, why don't you come too? We could play together.'

By now, my family were saying, 'We are going to find somebody for you to marry.' It was getting too much for me.

And then, slowly, we realised – why don't we both go, and start living there?

Escape

Jerry: But before that, someone had called and told the whole story to my father. When my family heard that I had a relationship with Sam, my brother and father stopped me from leaving home any more. No more sport. Nothing. And they beat me a lot. It was only when I went to the toilet, that I could use my mobile and talk to Sam.

I was waiting for my UK visa. When she was in Gujrat, she collected my passport and said, 'You've got everything now, including your visa.'

So we made a plan. One night, I ran away from the house and went to Gujrat. Next morning, I went to Dubai.

Sam: We went separately. I could not even go to pick her up. I did not say where I was going, just that I was going somewhere with the team. I left behind everything I had: my car, my bank cards, everything. So, we didn't have much money to travel.

Jerry: We thought if we went together it would not be good, they could catch us. And we didn't want them to know where we were going. I went to Dubai, and after two or three days she came. We spent about a week there and then went to Iran to meet our friend.

Sam: In Iran, we went to the holy shrine to pray. It's a sacred place of pilgrimage.

Jerry: After that we didn't want to go straight to the UK, because maybe they would find us. So, from the beginning, they were thinking we were still in Dubai. After Iran, we spent a week…

Sam: Changing places, going here, there, so they couldn't follow us…

Jerry: And after that, we came here.

Sam: But then, we did not know how to claim asylum.

Jerry: We didn't know anything about asylum.

Sam: We did not know that you can ask for help instantly, from the airport. And then later, at the interviews, they ask, 'Why did you not apply then?'

Jerry: For the first week we lived in a hotel in Ilford. But that was expensive. So then for a month we tried to find a room.

Sam: And then our money was gone. What could we do? We were on the street! We were living in the park.

Saved from the street

Jerry: Then a girl we knew in Coventry gave us a contact with a woman from an LGBT organisation called African Rainbow Family. She helped us a lot.

Sam: She picked us up from the street! She gave us accommodation while we put our case to the Home Office. That first day, she gave us a hotel room, then she took us to her own home for two days, and then we spent one week in the hotel. Her organisation helped us. It was really kind of them; otherwise, what would we have done?

Jerry: And so we went for our screening interview at Croydon. While we were waiting, they came in asking everybody, 'Why are you here?' Everybody who came to us said, 'Are you sisters?'

I said, 'No, she's my partner.'

'Oh. Okay, stay here.'

And I saw many women who had come in after us, going before us.

Sam: They were ignoring us. 'Oh, you are partners? Stay here.'

Jerry: Then we went in the queue and I said, 'We are partners,' and the official said, 'Not sisters? No? Go back and wait there.' She called other people.

Two or three hours we waited. Then the girl from Rainbow Family came. 'You still didn't get an interview?

I said, 'No, we are still waiting, and the people are treating us like this.'

Then she got angry with everyone and we got an interview.

We didn't ask for an interpreter, this woman just came. She was from Pakistan and she kept talking to the guy who was interviewing us, saying, 'How can they need asylum? They are rich people! Look at their phones, look at their clothes.'

Sam: She was saying we had expensive telephones. Because I was a successful sportswoman, I was wearing Nike sportswear, and she was saying, 'Oh, they look very rich. Why have they come here?'

Jerry: Then we tried to say, 'We came here to tell you our story. Please listen to us. We had a good life there. Why would we be asking for asylum if we didn't need it?

Sam: We had to leave my good career. I was earning money there – they were paying women players good money. And Jerry was about to get picked for the team. She had a good future there. Why do you think I'd leave?

Jerry: But she was trying to interrupt the guy who was interviewing us. I can still remember it. If I ever see that woman again, I don't know what I will say to her! After that we waited there for six hours. And then they rejected us. There, on the spot.

Sam: They do it to everybody. On the first attempt they don't give anybody the chance. They were not listening to us. And they did not give us accommodation. Then that lady who took us from the street... her boss shouted at them and sent a strict letter, saying, 'What are you guys doing?' Then we got a screening interview. She came with us and explained our situation.

'My bad time started from there'

Jerry: They moved us to a hostel for at least two weeks. They then said, 'You have to put in separate claims and you cannot share your room.' And we were like, '*What?*' They gave us separate rooms!

Sam: And the food was horrible. But still we were saying thanks to God, and thanks to the system over here. People who were behind these kind organisations, we were praying for them all the time. Then they sent us to Liverpool. They gave us a temporary apartment there, sharing with three or four other people. We had been given one room, we could cook there, and the lady used to come and give us money – five pounds! After that they gave us the letter that said we could find accommodation.

Jerry: That three months, it was the worst for me. My bad time started from there. We had left our money, car, everything in Pakistan – our life. And now this life, where we are waiting for five pounds! It was very hard. Sam went into a bad depression. I went to the toilet for one minute while she was in the kitchen cooking and I don't know what she did there, but she nearly started a fire and burned herself.

Sam: I told you before that when I was young, when my family put pressure on me, my mental health issues started. When I came here, it happened again. I was continuously thinking, we have lost everything: now what is going to happen? I was forgetting things, I was losing my memory, everything in front of me went black...

Jerry: When I was with her, sometimes she couldn't remember who I was. And sometimes she would treat me like an enemy.

Sam: They put us under too much stress. I nearly lost my mind.

Jerry: The worst thing was, I didn't know the language properly and couldn't explain everything. I tried my best. Even our friend from Coventry didn't help us. Sam had sent her six or seven hundred pounds, saying that when we come to England maybe we would need this money. But she stole it. She turned off her phone and didn't contact us. After that, the Home Office sent us to Rochdale.

Sam: We got a house in Rochdale. And I was fine, until the next decision came.

'They didn't believe us'

Jerry: At that time, we did not have a solicitor. We did everything ourselves. But Sam was not well. So, when we went to Liverpool for the long Home Office interview, I told them, 'My partner's not able to give an interview, she's not well.' But the GP hadn't given her a statement and they didn't believe me. Again and again, I told them, 'My partner is not well.' She was not ready to answer questions: when they asked her something, she talked about something else, and she laughed...

Sam: Then they gave us the decision: 'We cannot give you the status.'

Jerry: They said we were not partners, they did not like how we answered the questions, blah blah…

Sam: They were actually saying, you are not partners! Like, how can we prove that we are partners?

Jerry: From the beginning it was a big misunderstanding, from the first interview. Then, after they refused us, I found a solicitor, a legal aid one. He saw her and he understood. And he wrote a letter to the Home Office saying she was not well.

Then my solicitor prepared my case but again, the Home Office refused us, because they said we were not partners. So we appealed and went to court at Manchester. By then, Sam was worse. She could not go, but we gave evidence; a LISG member was there, and all the evidence was there. After that, they refused us again. They said they did not believe about Sam's condition.

After that, I was very sad. I was coming home with the bad news and crying all the way. When I reached home and saw the condition she was in – the worst she'd been – I tried to harm myself. I drank wine and then I tried to cut my wrists. I just felt like our whole life had gone. We didn't have a future any more.

But some LISG friends called me to see what the decision was, and one of our Asian friends came to our home, and she called emergency services. They took me to hospital. Sam started fighting with the police, saying, 'Why are you taking her?' because she didn't know what was going on.

For over a year I had been saying to the GP, 'Please refer her to some good doctor.' I told him again and again she was sick.

Then he said, 'Okay, she must take this pill and she will be fine.' She was not sleeping day or night; I was scared to leave her.

Sam: For forty-eight hours, I didn't sleep.

119

Jerry: And if she was standing somewhere, she was talking to herself.

Sam: My mind was stuck.

Jerry: She didn't remember anything and if she went out, she got lost. She would walk, walk, walk. She didn't know where she was going or how she would come back. Two or three times, we called the police and they brought her home.

'I am nothing here'

Sam: I tried to tell her. I said, 'When I was in Pakistan, there was a routine. I used to go to training first thing in the morning at nine o'clock. I used to get tired and then I would go to sleep. When I came here, my routine was upset. There was nothing, there was worry, and I was thinking, what's going to happen? Then I used to walk, walk, and I could not sleep.

Jerry: She didn't know where she was going or who she was talking to. One night, I tried to lock the door, but then I don't know what happened – I'd only been asleep a couple of minutes and suddenly I woke up and she was not at home. I tried to find her. It was night-time and, oh my God, I walked all over Rochdale and couldn't find her. I called Karen from LISG and she said to call the police, and they came. That whole night she was missing. I couldn't sleep all night worrying where she was, and the police were not telling me anything. In the morning two officers, one female and one male, came to the house and started checking everything. I was scared what had happened. I was very worried that someone had done something to her. (When we first lived here, someone threw eggs at our windows and wrote bad words, so I was scared a lot.) The police found her Pakistani International Driving Licence. They started looking at each other and said, 'What was she in her country?'

I said, 'She was a well-known sportswoman, and she

came from a good family, a rich family.'

Then they understood. They said, 'She is with us.'

Something had happened in a store. She was buying everything, as if, in her mind, she had a lot of money. I think she hit someone. And the store called the police. Then from there they took her to hospital. I told her story, that she was like this, and then maybe they contacted the GP. After four or five months, she was admitted to Bury Hospital under Section 3 of the Mental Health Act, and they started treatment. Then the social work team started looking at her and they helped us a lot.

I visited her every day and when I was watching her, I was crying. She was not like this in Pakistan. It was a very hard time.

Sam: Yes, it was a very hard time for us. I told her, 'I was trying to hide myself in front of you. Because, look, I am nothing here. I cannot do anything for you here.' So, I went into a deep depression. That was the worst time for me. I came out of hospital in 2017, and then slowly I got well.

'Two years they wasted for us'

Jerry: Then our solicitor left!

Sam: What happened was, when I was discharged, our lawyer was asking for my letters from the hospital, but it took six months to get them. Then he said, 'Okay, we will make the case.' But in March 2018 he said, 'I am leaving the law centre.' We got another solicitor, but it was July by the time she said, 'We've got the letters, you can come next month.' Next month, and next month... Then in September 2018, they said, 'We cannot take asylum cases any more.' Two years, they wasted for us!

Jerry: Then I searched for all the paperwork myself. I filed it all myself and someone told me to use a private solicitor. The senior solicitor was good. He said, 'Your case is good, they should give you the status.' But it was a junior who got our case and I was scared. He was thinking we had more money, but we said, we have just this little bit, and we borrowed some from a friend. I gave him all the paperwork, but someone had told me to make copies in case they mess up. And they didn't do anything. They just wrote a letter or whatever, but I prepared all the papers myself. Letters from the hospital, from LISG, from people who knew us very well...

Then he called us saying, 'We don't have Sam's records from the hospital' – the ones that took seven months to come! But I think he had hidden it. He hid a lot of papers. He said, 'I know a private doctor who will write one for you, they charge eight or nine hundred pounds, and they will have it for you within twenty-four hours.'

Sam: He thought we should make fake papers. No! If we have NHS papers, why would we need any private doctor?

'We always told the truth'

Jerry: At every step, we didn't tell any lies, we always told the truth. We don't like lies. I think he was trying for extra money, but I said, 'Listen. We have a copy we will bring tomorrow.' I showed him a picture of it on WhatsApp. When that junior solicitor had shown us our papers, the file was thin. But when we brought them all from home, he said, 'No need, I found all the papers.' And it was thick then!

But when we went to Liverpool, we found our solicitor had made one case for both of us.

Sam: They did not know the rules. You have to submit separate cases.

Jerry: Yes, when we went to Liverpool and gave them our file, they said, 'You are two persons, but your solicitor only booked one appointment for you.'

Oh! For three years I'd been struggling, struggling, and now, when we had an appointment for a fresh application, they said we would need to go back. I was crying and I said, 'I am so tired. We have come all the way from Rochdale, and our solicitors should know these things!'

Sam: Luckily, they said, 'Okay, we will do a photocopy of it all and put another title page separately.' So they put my name on the appointment as well, and we both did the interviews.

It was 26th March 2019 that we applied, and on 7th May we got the news that we had got our status! It was at Dallas Court in Salford – we used to have to go there to show we were present in the city. Every month, when you are still waiting, you go to sign.

Jerry: And if the Home Office reject you, they will detain you from there.

Sam: When we were leaving home that day to go and sign, I said to Jerry, 'I think they will say that you got the status.' And she said, 'You say that every time. Let's see.'

And that day, it really happened! The lady was sitting there and Jerry asked her, 'Please can you extend the date for next time?'

Jerry: 'Because we have had an appointment at Liverpool, so now you can give us two months before the next sign.'

And she said, 'Okay, let me check…' Then she said, 'Oh, Jerry, you don't need to come here any more, now you have got your status.'

She didn't understand what she'd said! I started crying. We were so happy! Then Sam started crying. I looked at her, and I was scared that maybe something bad would happen again. I was scared, because I couldn't bear another rejection.

Sam: But after a few minutes I said, 'Can you check mine too please?'

Jerry: And then they were very happy for us, because we'd been going there a long time and they knew us. We can't forget that day. It was a good month for us. It was Ramadan.

Sam: Yes, it was our holy month, and we were very thankful. We were thankful to the people who helped us.

Jerry: Especially LISG. When we were scared to go and sign, they were with us. And when Sam was at the hospital, they were with us.

Sam: LISG people helped us a lot. They were just like our family.

Jerry: After that, we applied to study. We have been at college this morning.

Sam: And in the future, we are planning to get married.

APHRODITE-LUNA

Unlike Sam and Jerry, the next two storytellers first came to England without any idea of settling here for good. Aphrodite-Luna wanted to travel, and had a sister here; later she returned to the UK as a student. At that point she could not have foreseen the events which would later make it impossible for her to return home.

Her story speaks to another painful truth of the refugee experience: the loss of home, family and country. However hostile, however abusive your family has been, to be rejected by them is one of the most painful things that can happen to anyone. Rebuilding your emotional support networks in that situation can be hard. For those who have been rejected by their biological families and might never see their parents or siblings again, 'chosen' family becomes of central importance. For Aphrodite-Luna, that support has come from the Metropolitan Church in Manchester, and from LISG. In those places, as she says, 'You are not alone, for they've got you, and you have found a family in them.'

I grew up in Nigeria in an extended family. As well as my siblings and parents, there were cousins and aunties who lived with us, because my parents were quite busy. They both worked in television: my dad was a producer and my mum was a creative director. Most times they were away. So I grew up under the care of an auntie, and there was always a cousin or extended family member in the house. I had five siblings, I'm the youngest. It was a very strict Christian background. Oh, yes! It was like, 'This is bad, this is bad, don't do this, don't do that!' It was always the *don'ts*, as opposed to what you *should* do. I went to a girls' secondary school, and it was always the don'ts: 'If you even *look* at a boy, you'll get pregnant!'

Growing up had its good moments, and it had its very bad moments.

I used to look forward to holidays, when we would go and see my grandmother. Because I was the youngest child, I was given extra attention – I never could do wrong in her eyes. It was a Christmas tradition that we go to my grandma's, because she lived in a village in the country-side. My sisters were the oldest, then there were three boys, then me. So I always used to play with my brothers. I used to play football, climb trees, and it was, 'Come down from that tree! You're a girl!' They would scold me and tell me I was supposed to behave like a girl. I never had dolls; I used to like cars and video games, and play football a lot. I think, initially, my mum didn't really pay any attention to that. I used to have short hair and look like my brothers: she would buy us the same clothes and a lot of people would think I was a boy.

That was okay until I got to a certain age. Then they started telling me, 'Oh you have to wear dresses, grow your hair, you're a girl.' I was a tomboy for the longest time, and at some point – I think when I was just entering puberty – they stopped letting me go out. Because my mum was always away, she'd say, 'You can't go out, you can't be in this boy's house.' So I was always at home.

But, before that… There was a cousin that was living with us. I think I was about eight or so, and he was an adult, nineteen or twenty, when he started abusing me. It started gradually. He used to tell me to touch him. There was just myself and my brother at home, and my brother was always outside playing football, so he'd say, 'Oh, come inside, you're not supposed to be outside.' That kind of thing. So he had access. For a while I didn't understand what was going on. It didn't make any sense to me. I summoned the courage to mention it to my mother and I got shot down. I wasn't sure why, but I think, for her, from this kind of African family, conversations like that are never had. And even if they happen, they try to hush it up. 'No, don't talk about it!' The second time I mentioned it – I was about ten – she beat me up. I think I fainted, I can't remember, and when I woke up she said, 'Never mention that kind of thing again! You can't be saying that, we can't be having this conversation!' After that, I didn't talk about it again. I couldn't tell anybody this was going on.

Boarding school

So when they said, 'Oh, you're going to boarding school,' it was freedom from what I was dealing with at home. I didn't like to come home, except if my siblings were going to be there. We had a week's break – they called it the summer week – and the option of staying at school. Some people went home, some didn't. I always opted for staying.

I had a bunkmate... I'd never been to boarding school, so I didn't know what to expect, but they pair you up with people a year or two older. I was in class one, and I think this girl was in class three. She was on the bottom bunk and I was at the top. I kind of got comfortable with her. She was two or three years older; we got very close and she taught me a few things! After a while, because it used to rain a lot – and it was loud, with thunder and lightning on a corrugated iron roof – you were allowed to go and sleep in someone else's bed. So, I used to come down and sleep in her bed, and things happened with her. That was my first experience with a girl. I liked it! I used to look forward to going back to school.

But that was why my parents took me away. They didn't find out, but there were rumours that things like that happened. My mother's friend had made a comment: 'Secondary school where you have only girls is not a good idea because they get to learn *all sorts of things* there.' And those were the things they used to preach against, because it was a Christian school. So, only a year later, I was taken out of boarding school.

Crushed

When they told me I was going home again, I was *crushed*, because I knew he was still living in the house and I'd have that to deal with. I tried to tell my mum that maybe she should give it another year; she'd see I was well behaved; she should ask my teachers. But her friend had already put that idea in her head; she was religious, and that's what they preached in church. 'Women sleeping with women? You don't want your children to learn that evil, cursed behaviour! You have to do everything you can to prevent it from happening!' And she bought into that.

When was I sent back home, my cousin continued with what he was doing. It was just me and him and my brother that were always at home, and I was growing up. I started puberty at about eleven, in boarding school; and when I came back and started to attend school as a day student, he got me pregnant. Twice: when I was twelve and when I was fourteen. My mother didn't know. He took me to a doctor – there were unlicensed doctors – and I had an abortion, on both occasions. I think, for a while, I was numb. I'd conditioned my mind to be numb to the things that were happening at home, because there was no other way of understanding.

One of my mum's colleagues had a daughter and I became friends with her. We were always in each other's company, so that was my only escape. She was an only child and they used to allow me to go to her house because she didn't live too far from us. We started to get really close, and she was actually the first person I kissed. We were always at theirs, and nobody suspected anything. They just said, 'They're like two peas in a pod,' and everybody was okay with that.

My cousin moved out of the house when I was fifteen. One day, I came back from school and they said, 'Oh, he's moving to another city.'

I was so happy! My siblings did not understand why I was excited that he was leaving. I was like, 'Is he going? Going and not coming back?'

'Yes, he's found a job and he's moving.'

I was still hurting from the fact that I didn't have anyone to tell what I'd had to deal with, but the fact he was going was enough for me. I thought, 'It's fine, he's leaving, he's leaving!'

It was a friendship bond I had with this girl. I don't know whether to call it a relationship. We were friends till I was sixteen and then they moved states. I was crushed when they were leaving. I didn't know how to be. I was kicking off at home and they didn't understand why I was so upset.

They said, 'Oh, you can always go there on holiday, maybe once a year.'

I said, 'I don't want to go there on holiday *once a year*! This is my *friend*!'

My mum said, 'Don't worry, you can always go and visit.'

But that never happened. There were no phones then, and it was rare to write a letter and have the person receive it. So I had that to deal with as well. It was like a big part of my life was just ripped out. I still remember, it felt like I had a physical pain in my chest for a long time. I was sixteen. I didn't do well that term in school: I had extra subjects that I failed and I had to go in during the holiday to write them again. Those were dark times for me.

Ordeal

I always used to mind my own business and I didn't really have friends. I would go to social events like someone's birthday, but I was a very quiet child. There was this boy who liked me and he didn't understand why I wasn't interested. He used to write me letters.

I told him, 'I'm not interested.'

And he said, 'Oh, why? I've never seen you with anyone.'

I said, 'My mother will kill me if she sees me with anyone.' That was the story I told them. But he still used to try. He would say, 'Oh, why don't we go for a drink? A date?'

And I would say, 'Don't you get it? I don't want to.'

He did that for quite a long time, till I was about nineteen.

One day – it was in May 2000 – I was coming back from church. We used to go every Sunday and my mum would stay most of the day. If my dad was around, he would go too, but he wasn't around that day. I was going past this boy's house and he said, 'Oh, how are you? I haven't seen you in a while.'

So I said, 'Yeah, I've been busy.'

He said, 'I've got the new Nintendo. Do you want to come and see it?'

I was into video games at that time, so I didn't think anything of it. Nothing bad crossed my mind. It was about nine or ten in the morning, I was just coming back from church, walking home.

He said, 'I can make you breakfast. We can play the game.'

And I thought, 'Yeah, cool, nobody's going to be at home anyway.' So I went into his house. His mum wasn't home; she and his sisters had gone to church, I think. I was sat in the living room, he made me fried egg and plantain, and I was playing the game and trying to figure it out. I was saying, 'Oh this is new, man! This is exciting, I like this!'

He was in the kitchen. Next thing, I could have sworn I heard him talking to someone.

I said, 'Is there anyone in the kitchen with you?'

And he said, 'Oh, my cousin is around, from university.'

I said, 'Oh, okay,' and continued playing.

After a while, he came and sat, played for a bit, went away, came back and sat down… He kept going back and forth, and I started getting uncomfortable.

So I said, 'I'm going to go in a bit.'

He said, 'Okay,' and he went to the door. I didn't know, but he had gone to lock the door and remove the key. Then he went back to the kitchen.

I got my bag, put on my shoes and said, 'Okay, I'm going to go now, I want to get home before my mother gets back.'

I went to the door and the key wasn't there. So I went to the kitchen and I realised there were more than two people in the house. There were four of them: himself and his cousin, and two of his friends. I was about eighteen or nineteen and these boys were about twenty-five.

His cousin said, 'So you're the girl he's been telling me about. You've been pushing him around! You don't like him. What is there about him that you don't like? Is he not good looking enough?' And stuff like that.

I just said, 'Let me go home.' I wanted to go through the back door.

And he said, 'Where do you think you're going?' He locked the back door, took out the key and put it in his pocket.

I started to beg. 'I need to go, my mother will be back home, she'll ask where I've been, I don't want to have to deal with that.'

Then he started pushing me around.

I was wearing a dress. Normally we'd wear dresses to church. So... So...

I can't talk about what happened next.

The ordeal lasted about three, four hours. Afterwards, I went home. Luckily there was no one at home. The only thing I was worried about – I wasn't even thinking about what had happened – was just, 'I don't want to be pregnant. I don't want to bring shame to the family.' So I went to the pharmacy and told them I'd had sex with someone and the condom had burst. That was what I told the pharmacist, because you have to explain, and he gave me a morning-after pill. And then I went home.

I used to see these boys now and then, and they would constantly threaten me, saying I shouldn't tell anybody what had happened. I think they suspected I was a lesbian. They'd never seen me with any guy. One had made a comment, 'If she doesn't like boys, she likes girls,' and I think it made them even angrier... Anyway, after eight months or so, I left home. I convinced my parents I was leaving to get into a federal university instead of a state university, but the real reason was that incident. And those boys threatened me until I left home.

'I did not refuse!'

In 2001 I moved to Lagos. One day I was in a shop and a girl was following me around. I asked her why and she said she liked something I was wearing. I told her where I'd got it from and we started having a conversation. I was waiting for my results, because you have to write an exam to get into uni, and we were waiting for the same thing. She was looking for a place to stay. I said, 'Well, you can come and stay at my place and we'll split the rent, if you don't mind.'

About two weeks later, she rang me. She'd thought about it and could we be housemates?

We became very good friends. I got into university; she got in, but later on that year. She came from another state.

One night, we were watching a movie and she said she'd never really had relationships with guys, she'd always had them with girls.

I found that quite interesting, because these are not conversations that you have, ever. So I asked, 'Why are you telling me this?'

She said she just felt she needed to tell me, in case I heard her talking over the phone to someone – that type of thing.

I'd already started to like her (I like full-bodied women, and she was very full-bodied) and I was attracted to her, but I couldn't let it show. So when I heard that, I just said, 'Oh, okay,' but in my head I was 'Yes!' I was ecstatic!

So, fast-forward to four months after I'd met her. I don't know what happened that night. We were in the living room, she came and sat down and was rubbing my feet... I never used to mind things like that, but because of how I felt towards her, it made me feel a certain way. She made a move, and I did not refuse!

So we came to an understanding. 'You know what this means. It must never leave the four walls of this house. As far as people know, we're housemates. You cannot tell *anybody* this is going on. Because I would deny it, I'd say I didn't know what you were talking about.' We had an agreement: whilst we were outside we were friends, whilst we were inside the house we were lovers. It made me compartmentalise. In front of my friends she was just my housemate, and in front of her friends I was just her housemate. Once her friends came round, I'd leave the house.

The truth is, I'd witnessed something when I was about seventeen, when they caught two girls, down our street. They brought them out and flogged them. Nobody gets involved when it's public punishment; people just stand and watch. Even if you call the police, the police come and *they* watch. Because they believe the community raises the child, you know. They stripped these girls naked and flogged them, and then somebody had some Scotch Bonnet paste, and they held the girls and put it inside them. So, imagine witnessing that experience! I was standing there! That gives you an idea. (Though it could have been worse – they believe in corrective rape as well.) I always had that picture of those girls in the back of my head.

And as I grew up, it got worse. I've seen that they caught two guys – people are very quick to react, 'jungle justice' is not frowned on – and they brought kerosene and doused them in it. They started telling them, 'You have to confess!' Someone standing by had a lighter and they were going to do it if the boys didn't promise to be a certain way. Someone was going to keep watching both of them, and if they suspected anything, they knew what would happen. And the parents were there – they were okay with that. Yes.

I explained all this to her, and she had seen things where she was coming from, so we needed to be super careful. There were no public displays of affection: I couldn't hold her hand outside, hugs were not longer than two seconds to be on the safe side, because I knew the likely consequences of people suspecting there was anything going on between us. It was not going to be pretty.

We lived together for about a year and a half, and then I think she got frustrated with not being more open. It wasn't entirely my fault, it was just how society thinks things should be. She wanted more, but I couldn't give her that. It started pushing us apart. I didn't want to be at home and she wanted me to be. I was getting angry as well, because I saw my friends in heterosexual relationships, how they were out there, and I couldn't do that. It was as if I was constantly choked. That's how I felt. And that affected the relationship, so that one day she just told me she was moving out.

I was hurt. I didn't think I was going to feel that way, but I was heartbroken! I didn't know what to do. It reminded me of losing the first girl I was with. I thought, 'Am I going to have to deal with those emotions again?' I wasn't ready for that. I started drinking a lot, smoking weed. I lived alone. I was trying to be brave: I'd tell myself it didn't matter. But when I'd go to bed at night, I used to cry myself to sleep – literally every day, for months. I lost so much weight that people were concerned.

Then my mum took ill and, after only six months, she died. That was in May 2003. I had all those emotions to deal with and I was grieving, so for a long time I didn't really date anyone. I couldn't even bring myself to like anyone, because I felt, 'If I like this person, they might go away; if I like that person, something might happen to them.' I grieved for a long time. And then a few years later my dad passed as well. It was a lot for me. What hurt most with my dad was that we were starting to be friends. I wasn't close to him, but I felt that even if he had found out I was a lesbian, he would have been okay with it. I think. He was open-minded. So, we were just getting to have a kind of father-daughter relationship, and then he passed. It was like everything rewound and started again. That was not a good seven years for me.

I was in my final year of university when I lost my dad. I had to take some time off, then I had an extra year to complete my course. I graduated in 2009 and plunged myself into work. I started as a customer service adviser, then after a year or so I started working in construction as a site supervisor. I was there for about two years, then I was a business development manager for about two years as well. And during that time, when I had a decent job, I didn't date anyone.

A lady from the north

I did meet a girl in 2012. I think ladies from the north of Nigeria are predominantly undercover lesbians! Those ones that wear the *abaya* and cover their hair, they're always supposed to be in the midst of other women, they're not allowed to be with men. The men marry them and then leave them at home with the other women. It's common knowledge, but nobody talks about it. So, when you meet a lady from the north, it's most likely that either she's bisexual or she's lesbian. It is known!

Her name was Didi and she came down to Lagos from Abuja. She was a business lady and we met at a Christmas party. She was very flirty. I thought it was the alcohol, but it definitely wasn't! I'd been out of a relationship for a long time and I wasn't actively searching, because I didn't feel I was at the point where I wanted anything serious; but I liked her. She walked into the room and I kept staring at her – yes, she was a full-bodied woman! And then she walked up to me and I thought, 'Oh shit, what's going on?'

She sat there and we started talking and talking, and spent the night just chatting and laughing and having a nice time.

She told me she didn't live in Lagos, but came in quite often from Abuja. I said, 'Oh, we should stay in touch then!' And we exchanged numbers and email addresses. Every time she was coming into town she'd let me know. At first there was nothing, but she was always very flirty. I just didn't pay any mind to it – deliberately. But one night, we went out, we had dinner, and after dinner we decided to go for drinks. And after that she said, 'Oh, do you want to go back home or do you want to come back to my hotel? We could continue the drinks there.'

And I thought, 'Wherever the wind takes us, I am going there tonight!' I just didn't care any more.

I'd known her about four or five months. We ended up in her hotel room. It had been a while, so it was all like fireworks. Everything was beautiful. And she said she was going to be coming back to Lagos very often. We kept seeing each other for a bit, and then she moved. I think she relocated to the States – the last time we spoke she said she was moving – but she kept in touch, and from time to time she reaches out. I spoke to her over Christmas.

A girl called Fury

So that was Didi. Then I started to travel. I think the first time I came to England was 2014. The company I was working for sent me here on a two-week training. I have a sister who lives in London: she's married with children and I'd never met my niece and nephew. She didn't know I was a lesbian; she wondered about me and thought I was strange, but never really questioned me. I told her I was going to come and see her.

So one day in 2014, I was on the train, going to my sister's house in Croydon, and I heard a girl talking on the phone. In Nigeria you speak English, but there's also 'broken English', and she was speaking broken English, so I thought, 'This person has to be Nigerian!' Then she said something in my mother's language, and I turned around and looked at her and laughed.

When she got off the phone, she came and sat opposite me and we started talking. I was trying to get to Victoria but I had got on the wrong train, to London Bridge, so she said she'd take me to Victoria Station.

We got to London Bridge and changed trains, and I asked her, 'Why are you being this nice? Nigerians are usually not this nice.'

She said maybe she'd just decided to, or maybe luck shone on me today!

We exchanged numbers and arranged to meet before I went back. We met up for a drink and we got on like a house on fire. So we kept in touch. We used to send WhatsApp messages back and forth when I went back to Nigeria, and when I came to England again, we saw each other. She told me she was a lesbian on the first meeting! And I was like 'Oh, right...' Because this wasn't something I was used to talking about, it wasn't a conversation I'd ever had, so it was brand new to me. If it happened by chance, which it always seemed to, then it happened. But she told me she'd had a girlfriend, she'd just got out of a relationship but she wasn't actively looking... And I never said anything.

When I visited in June, we spent time together and she asked me, 'Are you dating anyone?'

I said, 'No.' She never knew what to ask, because I was so used to masking it so that you'd never tell. I was used to not slipping up.

Then she asked, 'Oh, are you looking to date someone?' She just assumed I was straight.

After we got more comfortable with each other, I told her, 'You know I'm not straight, right?'

She was *ecstatic*. She'd kind of suspected, but she wasn't sure. She said, 'You're very good at hiding things.'

And I said, 'Well, I'm from Nigeria. What do you want me to do, let them kill me?'

Fury and I went on meeting every few months whenever I came to England.

'A normal relationship'

In 2016 I got a scholarship and moved to Manchester. I studied health and safety as an MSc and graduated in 2017. When I came to live in Manchester, Fury was living in London, but we could meet often. That was my first experience of a normal relationship. Initially, I still used to look over my shoulder – even now, sometimes I do. But for the first time, I was able to hold my girlfriend's hand in the street. She was surprised at my reaction because she grew up here, but I told her, 'You have no idea!' It was a new thing for me. It felt like freedom, release. I'd not experienced anything like that, so it was like a rush for me. I used to look forward to seeing her, just to hold her hand and not care. The day she kissed me at the train station – oh my goodness! I'm sure I cried that day.

She was wondering, 'What's wrong with you, why are you being so emotional?'

And I'm like, 'You wouldn't understand.' Because she used to do things like that – kiss me at the station – and she didn't understand why I would respond the way I did.

We dated until the end of '17. I started to understand that being a lesbian wasn't an issue here. And I started to get attention from women – a lot of attention! It was quite a rush. So every time she called me, she'd ask, 'Where are you?'

'Oh, I'm out having drinks...'

At first she was okay with it, but after a while it started to cause a problem, and it was, 'Who's that? Why is this person texting you? Why is this person calling?'

I never locked my phone, and she used to just pick it up and read through the messages: 'Who is she? Who is she?'

I said, 'I have nothing to hide. If you read the messages, they're just harmless, you know?'

But in a way I think that was what caused the relationship to end. She wanted me to move to London, to move in with her, but I said, 'Let me enjoy this new-found whatever-it-is, first!'

A nice girl

Before we broke up, I'd already met my current girlfriend. She was a friend of a male friend of mine in Nigeria. Before I left, every time he rang her, I also used to say hello. Her name was Bella. So I thought, 'When I go to England I'm going to meet up with her, catch up and have a drink.' I didn't know she was lesbian, I just assumed she was a nice girl, someone to catch up with in England. So after I came here, I did meet her, in 2015. I'd always told my girlfriend, Fury, that Bella and I were very close, but there was nothing between us. But Fury didn't like her: 'Who is she? Why is she always in your pictures?'

'She's just my friend!' To be honest I didn't even think about it initially; she was just a friend. There was a time I invited both of them out – it was a disaster. As soon as she arrived, I knew it was a bad idea.

After a while, our relationship was getting too stressful: Fury and I were always fighting, the arguments were getting a bit too much. I said, 'You know, I think it would be better if we just ended things.' I felt bad, because this was actually my first experience of having a proper relationship.

Bella was there for me and she's always been very supportive. She said maybe I should try again, and I said, 'No, I don't want to.' She held my hand through all the emotions and stuff.

I'd ended the relationship with Fury in October 2017. That Christmas, I went to London and met up with Bella at Euston Station. Neither of us was dating anyone. We were sitting outside having dinner and she was acting a bit funny, so I asked, 'What's wrong?'

She said she just had a bit on her mind.

I said, 'Okay, but you know you can talk about it?'

She said, 'Yeah, cool.' Then she just said, 'I don't know why we're not together.'

'What? With me?'

'Yeah.'

'You're sure you want to be with me? Me? You know me!'

She said, 'Yes, I know you, that's even more the reason why.'

'Wow. Listen, are you sure it's not the red wine talking?'

But she said no, she'd been thinking about it a lot, and she knew that if she let this opportunity pass, I would soon be in another relationship and then she'd have to wait.

I said, 'Have you been waiting then? Wow, you didn't tell me! Look, I don't plan to date anyone. But I need you to think about this, if this is what you want. You know me, and you know the drama that comes and goes with me.'

And she said, 'Yes, it's not about that.'

So I said, 'Okay!'

And we've been together since 2017.

'Back-to-back hate'

In 2018, I came out to my brother. I think it was a year after we'd started dating. I was tired of hiding, because when I went back home to Nigeria – I visited home a few times when I was studying, twice or three times – it was always, 'When are you going to get married? Don't you think you're getting too old? Don't you want babies? Don't you want this, don't you want that?'

I'd say, 'Don't worry, we'll talk about that.' And I'd stay one week and I'd be out!

I started hearing conversations within the family that there was someone they'd arranged for me to marry. He was a doctor from a good family. They'd met with his family and I just needed to come back home so they could make proper arrangements and have a ceremony. Truth be told, as a woman, you're seen but you don't have a voice. They don't want to know what is in your head, they just make arrangements for you. And that started to scare me, because I'd seen it happen to my cousins. It's a normal thing. They marry you off and that's the end: you can get to know the person while you're married. And none of those marriages, as far as I know, have worked. I know because they told me.

So, I came out to my brother. I sent him an email. I couldn't tell him on the phone because I didn't know how. He was my closest sibling. He didn't respond at first, it took him about two or three weeks, though normally we'd talk every day. I didn't know if he didn't know how to respond to the email, or if he didn't understand what I'd just said.

He responded eventually, and he was like, 'Oh, I don't know what to say really because I don't understand. I still need time to think about what you've just told me.' He had been thinking that once I'd finished studying, I'd come back home and settle down. 'Because that's what's expected of you, everybody's waiting, you're the only girl left that's not married.'

I said, 'Okay, fine, if you need to think about this, think about it and let me know. Because it took me a while to tell you.'

I'd been with my girlfriend for a year and I just thought, 'You know what? Instead of hiding and going and coming back, just tell them. The earlier they start dealing with this, the better. I know not everybody will be pleased, but let the shit hit the fan, and then we can start cleaning up the mess early as well.'

Then, I don't know what happened. I think he told my older brother. And my older brother told my cousin – *the* cousin. In my family, they have like a hierarchy of men, so every generation has a representative, and that cousin is currently the oldest male grandchild. He runs the show. When they heard, it was phone call after phone call after phone call, and text message after email after phone call. It was just back-to-back hate.

'Come back home. We will deal with you. Come back home. You will be punished, you will be fined, we have notified who we need to notify, and once you step through the airport, we will get you. You cannot hide.'

When those messages started coming in, it started to stress me out. I was ready to go home, I swear. In 2018, in April, I was ready to go home. Because it was just like *bam, bam, bam, bam,* and the pressure was so much. I thought, 'At least they're not going to kill me.' That's what I was telling myself!

My girlfriend said, 'Are you *sure* you want to do this?'

I'd bought my ticket! I still have the ticket today. I went to the airport. I just didn't get on the plane. I did not get on the plane, because I thought, 'What am I doing? Is this the right thing to do?' Sometimes I do act before I think. I didn't get on the plane, but I didn't know what to do.

They were calling, asking, 'When are you landing, when are you landing?' They knew when the plane was leaving, so they were expecting me to come.

And I just got on a train and went to my sister's house. I said, 'Look, this is the situation,' and I told her.

She was shocked. First of all, it was, 'I don't want you to come to my house and teach my children anything!'

I said, 'Okay, I'm not teaching anybody anything. Children learn more outside than they learn inside the house.'

She said, 'Those are the conditions to be in my house.'

And I said, 'That's fine.'

So at least I had some kind of respite at hers. I thought, 'Okay, I'm going to be here for a while till I decide what to do.'

But I didn't know what to do. I had no idea there was anything like asylum: no idea! My visa had expired. I did go to the Home Office in May 2018. I stood across the road, thinking, 'Do I just walk in?' I was supposed to have left that April and I didn't. I thought, 'If I walk in, I'm going to be arrested!' I was so afraid.

I didn't have an idea what to do, and I was getting these messages from home. 'Don't come back if you're not ready to deal with this! What kind of news are we hearing? What is this behaviour? Your parents would turn in their graves, they'd be so ashamed of you!'

They started trying to use emotional blackmail. My auntie rang. She said she'd heard, she'd been sick, her blood pressure had gone up, I should come back, we should have a conversation.

So it was always, 'Come back, come back, come back!' That's all I was hearing.

And after a while it was, 'Oh, you're making Auntie sick. If she dies, her blood is on your head.'

This went on for a good six months. I wasn't eating, I wasn't sleeping, I was just existing. And I couldn't stay at my sister's any more, because they kept calling her, so I thought, I'll go back to Manchester.

Dark times

I came back to Manchester and I put up with a friend of mine. She used to work in Leeds, so she was hardly ever home. I went to the GP and told him I wasn't sleeping at all, and he gave me sleeping medication. One day – I don't know what happened, I think I'd just had enough – I took an overdose. I was hoping something would happen. I think I slept for three days. My friend would usually go to work on Monday morning and come back on Friday. So I was home alone and I did that. When I woke up, I was kind of disappointed.

I went to the GP and told him, 'Look this is the problem: my family have found out about my sexuality and I don't know what to do, so this is what I did.' He arranged for a mental health assessment, but that took a while. He arranged therapy for me as well. I'd never had therapy before; I didn't know what it was. It was alien to me, because talking about problems back home, they frown on it; there's nothing like therapy there. The first time I went, it was a man. I felt very uncomfortable, but I didn't know how to say it. By the third week he referred me to the LGBT Foundation, because he felt there was more to this than he was trained to handle. I had no idea this building was in Manchester! They booked me for an assessment – that took a while, as well, because there was a waiting list – and then I came here, to the LGBT Foundation.

For the first few weeks I couldn't say anything, because I didn't know what to say. You know, sometimes I'd just sit for the hour and then I'd go home; then the next week I'd come back for the hour, twiddle my fingers, go home. It took a while before I started to tell the therapist what was going on. Then, it was like years of everything bundled up and then let out. It was a lot. Sometimes there were weeks when I didn't want to come back. I kind of felt ashamed, because these were conversations I'd never had with *anybody*. I'd ask, 'Is it safe? Is it safe?' I hoped she wouldn't report me... I still struggle with all that, you know.

I changed my phone number after it got too much. After the suicide attempt, I changed my address as well, so they couldn't reach me. Even my sister doesn't know my address; none of them knows where I live. They'd started to send her letters. They wrote a long letter to her, saying that whenever she finds me, she should give it to me. It said: 'We've disowned you; you're no longer one of us; you've brought shame to the family; you're a curse; you're a disgrace; you're a sin.' There was nothing that wasn't said! 'Your parents would have spat in your face if they'd found out this shameful thing you're doing. It's disgusting.' I had so many messages from back home, from different people: people I knew, people I didn't know, everybody had a say.

I had no idea what else to do. I was so pressured. I woke

up one day and I walked to the tram stop – I don't take trams, I don't know what took me there – but I was like, 'Maybe if I just walked under the tram? It would be okay, and everybody would be fine.'

There was a lady there who asked me, 'Are you okay?' I was standing at the edge of the tram platform and she said, 'Are you okay?'

'I don't know.'

So she just held my hand and pulled me back. I don't know who she was.

And these are things I never imagined I would do. When I hear of people wanting to harm themselves, I think, 'How could you think of that?' When I got home, I thought, 'This is me, thinking of doing this!'

I didn't know who this lady was. She gave me the Samaritans, or some phone number, so I called them, then I didn't know what to say. I was on the phone for like, forty-five minutes, didn't say anything and hung up. But I called them the next day, and after a while, I'd call them during the week and then, on a Friday, I'd go for therapy. I'd call them during the week, and that helped me balance the waiting till Friday.

Then my girlfriend said, 'I think you should speak to a lawyer who could advise you on what to do.'

Seeking asylum

The lawyer said, 'Listen. These are obvious threats to your life. If you go back home, what if they kill you?' He advised me to seek asylum and that's when I did it.

You go to Croydon for an assessment. Mine was on 10th January 2019. The Home Office called me for interview two weeks ago, in February 2020. So I'd waited a year! They haven't said anything just yet, but the interview was quite different from what I was expecting. You have to sign a consent form for them to access your medical records. The woman told me she'd seen that I made a suicide attempt, and she knew it's a sensitive subject, but I should make sure that I follow it up. She told me there's a counselling session for rape or trauma, regardless of how long ago, that runs for twenty-six weeks, and she said I should make sure I attend every one of them. Well! I went there afraid, after what I'd heard about them, but she was telling me I should follow up with those appointments, and she would make sure the safeguarding team contacted me. This was quite different from what I was expecting. I'd heard a lot of stories from different people, how they come with fire and spears, ready to eliminate or kill, or say you're lying. But she just said, 'Make sure that you attend each and every one of these things. Don't miss anything.'

I gave them all the evidence. I had to make screen shots of the messages I was receiving from home, I had to give them that letter saying all sorts of frightening things. There was so much to give them! I gave them all that. I think they do understand about Nigeria. They know. So that's where I'm at. Normally, they respond within two weeks, but they haven't said anything yet.

'There's a lot of love'

What am I doing now? I'm still living with my friend, and she's hardly ever there, so that's fine. I do a lot of volunteering... that's all I do. Where I volunteer, there's a church, and they have a food bank at the church every week.

When I found out about the Metropolitan Church, I didn't believe at first that a church would accept me. I used to sit right at the back – just in case I needed to run. I would go every Sunday and sit at the back, but as time went on, I started to get comfortable. They were very open and affirming. There was nothing like, 'You will die if you do this. In Leviticus, the Bible says a woman must not lie with a woman...' That's all I heard as a child, that's all I heard growing up. Even at home, they used to make general comments, not that they suspected anything, but like, 'Oh, this person's daughter is going with this person's daughter, they will burn in hell!' or 'This is a sin!' So finding that church for me was like, 'What? An LGBT church?' If I remember clearly, back home there was someone that attempted to start such a church. They burnt the building down.

They asked me, 'Are you going to come next Sunday?'

'Yeah, I'm going to come!'

They let you understand that you're welcome without judgement. The door's always open, whenever you want to come. There were no hang-ups, no awkward bits, it was just, 'Come in!' And they make you feel at home. Sometimes when I sit in church, I'm like, 'Wow, this is actually true, it actually exists!' Everybody makes you feel welcome; you don't feel like you're out of place. It's a mixed crowd. Now, I sing in the choir, I take part in the cleaning up after the service. They have refreshments and then we make sure we clean up and tidy up before we go home. You build a bond, you build friendships. It's like a family for me.

When you go to Croydon for your screening, they give you leaflets. I think the first leaflet I saw was for the UK Lesbian and Gay Immigration Group, which was in London. But that was when I realised there were support groups. I didn't know before that. I went online, checking for groups in Manchester, because going to London for a support group didn't make any sense. I started going to First Wednesday, and they told me about LISG.

I've been with LISG for about a year. I don't know what I would have done without LISG! Because it was then that I found out it was not just me on this journey. There were other people who had different issues and came from different countries, but had a similar story. These people were struggling like myself, with acceptance from family, and other things as well. LISG has just held my hand ever since. I look forward to going to meetings, I try to get involved as much as I can. There are some people that are very vulnerable in LISG, as well; we just carry each other along. There's a lot of love and you know that if you cry, somebody will respond. You never feel like you're by yourself. You are not alone, for they've got you and you have found a family in them.

~

Aphrodite-Luna told me her story at the end of January, when she was still waiting for the decision on her asylum application. Three weeks later, she heard that yes, she had been granted her refugee status. However, even that news was not final, because the Home Office can appeal against a judgement within two weeks: another stressful wait. So it was not until early March that the rest of the group learned the joyful news that Aphrodite-Luna really had 'got her stay'.

FAITH

Like Aphrodite-Luna, Faith came to England to study. She intended to return home to Africa afterwards, even though she loved the freedom that LGBTQ+ people enjoy in the UK. When the one person she trusted 'outed' her to her family, going home suddenly became impossible. Faith found herself, like many other refugees, with an expired visa and no one to turn to for advice. With the love and support of her girlfriend ('She's my rock'), Faith has finally completed the asylum process and now they can begin to build their life together in the UK.

I've always been a tomboy, maybe because I was the only girl in the midst of three boys. I used to take my dad's clothes and my brothers'. My dad did most of our shopping, because he was always abroad, but he was not the kind that would go from shop to shop. He would just go into one shop and be like: 'Give me four of those. Give me four jeans! Give me four tops!' So that's why I had mostly boys' clothes – black, white and grey – and I fell in love with those colours. My mum, on the other side, wanted me to wear pink and all of that. I used to say to her, 'Why would I be so girly? I don't like being girly, it annoys me. I want to be free.' The boys were free to do anything. But I always had to do my hair...

One day I said, 'Do you know what? Just cut this hair! I'm not doing my hair any more.' So all through high school, I had a low cut. I was very boyish, very free. I wasn't much of a basketball player, because I'm not tall like my brothers, but I was into video games. At the time, I didn't know I was being boyish, I just thought that was normal. And my father was very liberal, and anyway he was not around so much; Mum was the one that was mostly at home.

Dad is a Muslim, Mum's a Christian, but Dad was very liberal in those days. He's an engineer and he worked in France and Italy, and he's well read. My mum was an accountant. We all went to boarding school – it was the norm, I would say. My parents feel that's where you get your independence. You're 'babied' at home; you go to boarding school and get sharp. I was in boarding school for six years. I was a bright kid and quite ambitious. The best years were the last three, because I became a house prefect, so I was in charge of my house. Yeah, it was good.

First Love

There was this girl, Joy. We started off just friends. By the end of junior studies three, we started to visit each other during the holidays – she didn't live far from school, and I lived really far away. We became very close and by the second year of senior studies we went everywhere together. We were in the same class. Joy became an acting prefect, and I was acting prefect for my house – so that's when the relationship started, because we were free, no one was watching us, I was in charge of the hostel. It wasn't something that was planned, or that we spoke about – it just happened. I was happy. She was the first person I'd ever been with and I didn't understand what was happening. In fact, it was shocking. I remember when the Home Office interviewer asked me about it, I said to him, 'It wasn't something we discussed at all, we didn't say, "I love you..." No, that was not the situation.'

We were fond of each other, we did everything together. Boarding school is restrictive, so we had breakfast at a certain time, school at a certain time, everything at a certain time. When she was a prefect, we would leave the hostel together and go to her duty post, but I was lacking in my duty post, because the hostel was not as clean as it should be. So I was called out, and we stopped doing that. But, literally, we would do everything together: we sat together in class, wrote exams together. When we kissed, I didn't feel she was going to slap me, I didn't feel like there was going to be any bad outcome. I trusted her.

Even after it happened, we didn't talk about it. She was a bit shy. One time I just said, 'I enjoy kissing you,' and she said, 'Me too! But you know it's wrong.' We used to sleep together: I was on the top bunk and Joy was on the lower bunk. At that time, if you saw two girls together, nobody suspected anything. Unlike now! I tried to explain that to the interviewer, too, but he didn't understand. It was normal. There was just one time... I think we had finished high school and she was already at uni. She came to my house and we met up with some friends – we were going to the cinema or something – and we held hands. We were out on the street, and one guy said, 'Why are you holding hands? Leave her hand alone!' I quickly removed my hand. I remember that. That was the first time anything like that ever happened. Before that, it was not the case.

Those were happy times. I didn't know what I was doing. I'd not seen any films or books about lesbians, but I liked her being around. She had perfect breasts as well. So yeah, I just liked her and didn't get to thinking more deeply.

Heartbreak

The girls attended separate universities. Joy's institution was stricter and she was in a hostel with about a dozen other people. Faith visited her there frequently and people accepted that they were best friends; but Joy still worried about being found out.

I remember one time, we were kissing and everything, and Joy stopped me. She said, 'I tell you, we can't do this.'

I said, 'Why?'

'If they catch us, we're finished. And you can always go back, but it's my school.'

We were just lying there, and I said, 'Don't you want me to continue?'

And she said, 'I want you to continue, but we can't risk being caught.'

We'd got caught once in high school, but this was on a different level. So I said, 'Okay.'

That was the last time I went there. I didn't want to put her in trouble, because it would be worse for her. I could run away, but she couldn't. So I just stopped visiting. We only saw each other when we were on holidays after that, or when she was at home.

Joy and I planned to move abroad for our master's degrees, so we could be together, but my dad wanted me to gain work experience first. So she went on to study for her master's and I stayed back to get work. She was getting pressure from her parents, saying she needed to marry, because she's the second girl and the eldest had already got married. I travelled to visit her and there was this guy who was always coming to see her. And she lied to me. They'd been at the same university and she said, 'Oh, he's my friend.' I'd always heard his name – he was quite a brilliant guy – and I just thought she wanted to share with someone who was bright. I didn't know that they were having something together. After I went back, I tried calling her, and that's when I realised.

When she told me, 'Oh, I'm seeing him, by the way,' I was devastated. It was over the phone.

I couldn't believe it. I was still in denial. I was like, 'You can't do that!'

I remember her crying. I was on the landline, the phone in the house, so I couldn't be too... Yeah, sad times. So long ago.

She got married after university and we officially ended things, but I think I was still living in denial. I felt, 'No, we still have a bond.' I'm a believer in bonds: I feel there are some things you experience with people and those people will be in your life forever. That's the kind of person I am. And I didn't want to believe she would forget. I would check up on her and we would talk. Then I came to England and, you know, it felt like I was the one doing most of the calling.

She'd still pick up my calls, but not as frequently as back in the day. I thought, 'Okay, I'm going to focus on my studies.' But she was not only my girlfriend, she was also my best friend. She was someone who knew everything about me. I had friends, I was quite popular, but she was the only one who knew a hundred percent of me. The secrets I had were with her. She was the only person I could speak with, without being judged.

When I think how bright I was when I was young... I loved studying, I loved doing research, I had drive. I felt, 'I'll come to England and the sky's my limit!'

And then it all crumbled.

England

I came to England to study for my master's degree. I saw girls kissing on the streets. I thought, 'Uh-oh, this is the life! I want this.' But I didn't know the rules, or what to do. When I'd go to class there was nobody who stood out to me like a lesbian – to be honest, I didn't even know how to spot anyone.

One time, my flatmate said, 'Oh, my sister's coming over from Hungary.' (She was studying there.) So her sister Alice came. She was very nice, very friendly – I got on with the sister more than the flatmate. She was very tactile – when she joked or laughed, she touched me. There was something, but I didn't have any gay radar, so I didn't know what was going on. Besides, she was from my country, and you have to be very careful or before you know it, your news is everywhere!

She would come to my room, sit on my bed and hang out with me, more than with her sister.

'Oh, Faith, what are we watching? Let's watch something together! Let's share a duvet!'

She'd come and sit next to me on the sofa, we'd use the duvet together, but there was not any... We'd just stay there.

I was thinking, 'This girl, she's too friendly,' but then, it was nice. She went back home, but she would call: 'Oh, I miss you so much!' And we'd talk.

Questions

So all this was playing in my head. I had a friend, Mark. He didn't know my family, so it was easy to tell him stuff. He was a nice guy and we had things in common – we both liked tech – so it was easy to say, 'Guess what happened? Do you think I should say this?'

He said, 'Just ask her, what's the big deal?'

And I'm like, 'Oh, man! I can't. You don't understand.'

'Just ask her, you never know.'

So I asked Alice, 'Why did you touch me like that, why did you do this and this?'

And she said, 'You look to me like you're a lesbian.'

I said, '*You* look to *me* like you're a lesbian!'

'Are you?'

'Let me ask you first! Are *you*?'

Then she said yes, she was. And I said yes, I was.

She told me she knew from day one! 'I just knew it!' She'd been abroad way before I had; she knew, straight up. So that was how that started!

She used to come and visit about twice a year. But I quickly realised she was bisexual, and it was just something I didn't want. I didn't want to be with a girl who's with a guy. She was clear with me: 'I'm going to get married to a guy, because of my family. Otherwise my dad's going to cut me off and I don't want that to happen.' She enjoyed being with a girl, but she was still going with guys. And she loved all the attention.

My idea was, you'd be friends first, then you start dating and are loyal to each other. I was not used to someone having other people too. So that was my ideology: you're faithful to each other. But with Alice, it was different: every time I saw her, I didn't know where she'd been, what she'd done. I used to struggle with that a lot. But it was either that or nothing, and I did like her.

Mark knew all about that, and I would tell him my displeasure: 'Look at what she's doing! She's gone to this place, that place, and she's telling me, "Oh, there's nothing with this guy," but he bought her this...'

So he knew all this, and he would advise me, 'Be mad at her!' But I didn't know how to do it. I wasn't very vocal anyway, I wouldn't chat with people. I would chat with Mark more than other people. I'm good with writing, but I was not very expressive. I think maybe it's a cultural thing. Back then, I couldn't sit with someone and talk about my life like I'm doing now. No way. I think it was how we were brought up – even though I was brought up differently, to be fair – but a woman's place is in the kitchen. I don't want to say we were intimidated, but a woman doesn't speak out. I struggled with that for a while; I'm still working on it.

So that was the story with Alice. It was quite short, but it was fun. We'd go out. I remember her sister would sometimes get guys to take us out. I wouldn't want to go, but Alice would say, 'Oh no, let's go! I'm only going with you really, you know!' And we'd go out, but obviously we would not be seen together in public, we'd not do all of that – we never even kissed in front of her sister. Alice was crazy, you know, and I wanted someone who was soft, easy-going, calm. I'm very calm, I don't like all that drama... but it was fun. It was something to look forward to, when she was coming.

Up his sleeve

I need to tell you more about Mark now, and that's the most painful part of my life. Mark was the first person I met when I came here. He's Portuguese. I met him at the cinema – I love movies. He asked me why I was on my own and what I was going to see, and we watched *Happy Feet 2* together and exchanged numbers, and I felt I had made my first white friend! I think it was during the festive period, because I remember the cinema was all decorated. We kept in touch, we would talk, he was a very wise guy. I had a Blackberry phone – the flip one, white, which was not common then. He had a normal one and every time I brought mine out, he was like, 'Oh, I want to see your phone!' I think that's what attracted him to me, maybe! So, we'd talk about gadgets, what's going on, school... We were friends.

Then he started saying I was miserable, and that it seemed to him I was the kind of girl that wanted to settle down and have a home. He knew all about my problems with my girl-friend, and he would tell me, 'That's how girls are in this country, you can never have anyone loyal.'

I believed him, because I didn't know his intentions. I didn't know what he had up his sleeve. I believed all that he was saying.

'Girls in England, that's how they are. Nobody's going to stick with you. You can't have a faithful relationship. You seem like you want someone that's there for you, someone you can come home to, and you can't have that with the girls in this country, blah blah blah...' And before you know it, he was asking me to be his girlfriend.

Well, I was like, 'Are you having a laugh? Are you drunk? What's the problem?' That was the first time I had seen him like that.

But he said, 'Honestly, I've liked you from day one.'

It did feel really strange, as I never pictured myself with a man and was not attracted to him in that way at all, but he was so nice to me. He knew about Alice, but he said it was a phase I would grow out of and I could never settle down or have a family with a lesbian, which was what I wanted.

Mark also knew that I was getting pressure from home. My dad was saying, 'You're the right age. I want you to get married to a Muslim guy. There's a guy I want you to get married to at home.' My dad had always been a Muslim, but we were not forced to do anything when we were young.

I even used to wear jeans. Once in a while, we would go to the mosque. He would tell us, 'You need to pray,' but he wasn't strict. Then, all of a sudden – I think especially when we moved cities – he joined a Muslim community and gradually became one of the elders. He was sucked into it. He started to give my mum pressure as well, because she's Christian. He became too religious; he became horrible. So, he was putting pressure on me to get married to someone he had chosen, who I did not know, and my mum didn't know either – from the community he'd joined. My mum was saying, 'No way! I made a mistake in my life, and I will not let any of my children make that mistake!'

Mounting pressure

So, I got scared of what was happening at home and it started to affect my studies. I used to speak to my mum more than my dad. He was like a dictator: whatever he said was final. We couldn't argue with him or stand up to him; we didn't have the courage. I remember when I was going to school, to ask my dad for pocket money, I would stand in front of the mirror and say, 'I need this,' practising beforehand. It was like that.

And now Mark was putting pressure on me as well. At that point, I said, 'You know where I stand.'

He said, 'But we're very close. We speak more than two, three times a day' – which was true – 'I know everything about you, you know everything about me, we motivate each other. I don't see me being with anyone else, and I don't see you having the life that you want.'

I said, 'But I've never been with a guy, I've never dated a guy.'

'It's just flesh, it's nothing, it's all about the soul! I'll teach you how to love me.' That's what he said. 'You know you already love me as a friend, so the rest is easy.'

So I thought, okay.

157

I was enjoying our going out together and stuff like that. I felt I had a friend. I had left the Church, so I had no other friends. He was just there, and I felt, 'Okay, it's not like anything extra. We're just friends.'

More than friends

There was so much pressure. I was finishing at university and was going to have to go back to my home country. In those days, I didn't know much about visas. When I was coming here, an agency did the visa application, so in my mind it was just part of coming to England to study. I knew that if you came on holiday you needed a visa, but I didn't know what the visa for marriage was, or anything. When I had to extend my student visa, the school did the extension. Mark was more knowledgeable. He said, 'Oh, you will have to go back, and then you're going to have to get married to the Muslim guy.'

Obviously, I really didn't want that to happen, but I didn't know *how*.

Then, one day, he proposed. He came to the house where I was living and asked me to marry him. It was a surprise to me, I didn't expect it. We had a long talk. He knew I fancied girls and was scared of going into marriage with him.

I remember asking him, 'How are we going to live? You know I'm still attracted to girls.'

And he said, 'But you've not been happy with any of them. Only with me!'

Which was true.

I remembered my mum saying to me, 'I want you to get married to your best friend.' And at that time, I thought, 'Who's my best friend? Mark!' And he did know everything I was going through.

So I just agreed. I thought, 'Okay, this will be easier for me.'

I didn't know what it would be like, but he said, 'I'm not

going to rush you. I'm not going to do this, I'm not going to do that...'

And I said, 'Okay.'

When I told my mum, she said she was glad I was going to marry my best friend, someone I had chosen for myself; but my dad was furious, saying he knew nothing about Mark and I was going against his wishes. Eventually he came round, because Mark promised he would not interfere with my religion.

We got married. I was studying at the time and I was in a tenancy, so I kept my apartment and Mark lived with a friend near his work, while we waited for our interview for the council house he had applied for. He would mostly come around to mine when he was off work. I dreaded it, because he kept asking for sex. I was so scared to have sex with him. I did not even want to see him naked. Every time was a different excuse from me: either I was on my period or I was too tired and wanted to sleep. This got him really frustrated, and made us argue almost every day. I felt sorry for him, and tried my best to be a good wife to my husband, but I just could not satisfy him sexually. I gave myself to him on a few occasions, after drinking, and hated every bit of it.

Making connections

A few months later, I ran into an old friend of mine, John – we'd attended university together. He became a good friend. He's gay and I was able to share with him all that had been troubling me. He told me he never felt proud as a gay man until he came to the UK. He said that once I got familiar with the LGBT community, I would feel better, because I'd meet like-minded people. It was John who introduced me to the LGBT Foundation, and I started attending and volunteering at events, which introduced me into the community and LGBT life. Whenever Mark was not around or we'd argued, I would go out to particular bars I liked. I used to get quite a lot of attention from women, both lesbians and those who were bi-curious; we would have casual encounters, but it never developed into anything serious.

One Tuesday, I was at a social group for women at the LGBT Foundation and we were watching a movie titled *Imagine Me and You*. It was about a lady, Rachel, who was engaged and about to wed, but met a woman she had an instant connection with. She was torn between sticking to the norm (getting married) or following her heart to be with this lady. Rachel was so miserable and constantly fighting a battle within herself. I could connect with her instantly and relate to so many aspects.

Soon after, I decided to sit Mark down and tell him how I felt, how I was sure of my true sexual identity and how I could not hide it any more. I explained it would be unfair on him to continue this marriage because my heart was not in it and I had never felt happier than when I was attending the groups and meeting people who understood me, where there was no hiding.

He was so angry. He made horrible remarks and threatened to inform my parents. He knew that my country is homophobic, so he said if I left him, he would shame me and my family. I was sad to have hurt someone who loved me, but I could not help feeling relieved everything was out in the open. That was when Mark informed my parents, via Skype, about my sexuality. He told them I was always on the phone talking to girls, and disrespecting him. My mum called me and cried on the phone, saying I had brought shame to the family and that Mark had threatened to expose me and shame my family if I did not go back to him.

Mark later told me that he had sent them copies of intimate photos, messages and Valentine cards I had exchanged with other females. I do not know how far those pictures have circulated. I did get some threat calls from home, from strange numbers, so I had to change my number and Skype details. My father said he never wanted to set his eyes on me again and that the day he does, he will kill me. I was so scared and troubled. I did not know what to do. I would cry and could not eat for days.

I started going to a group called First Wednesday, where they tell you how the asylum process works. At first, I didn't even know what asylum was. It's very helpful, they tell us the experiences people have had, and people can share their stories. People would say, 'Oh, I was interviewed, and this happened...' But I couldn't tell my story. I just couldn't. I remember I would just sit at the back and listen to these horrible stories, how people got locked up in detention and stuff like that. I didn't want that to be me. I didn't think I could do it. So there was that fear as well. I'm very good at just brushing things under the carpet; I don't like to talk about bad stuff, or see people moody. I just don't like too much serious stuff. And I was so scared, I felt I couldn't go through it. It was Natalie, my present girlfriend, who finally encouraged me into it.

New love

I met Natalie in 2015. I was at a social group at the LGBT Foundation, and there was this girl who caught my eye. On this fateful day, we watched that same movie, *Imagine Me and You*!

I remember Nat saying, 'Ah, that movie touched my heart.' She had tears in her eyes.

Well, I couldn't stay in that, so I walked away. I don't like to see anybody in dismay. But she was saying it to get my attention, so she thought I was absolutely rude.

Later on, she was using her phone to take pictures. She said to me, 'Oh, look at this picture of you!'

I said, 'Send it to me!'

And of course she said, 'Can I have your number?' That was her plan, that's why she used her phone to take the pictures.

So we exchanged numbers and she sent me the pictures, and after that she would call me up saying, 'What are you doing today, what are you doing tonight?'

I was always coming up with an excuse, because I knew there was a girl that liked her, so I didn't want to be in their way. I just wanted to be friends with everybody, that's my style.

Anyway, Natalie kept on and I thought, 'Oh, my days!'

I remember one time that she called me. It was raining and she said, 'Where are you?'

I said, 'I've just had my hair done, tightened up my locks, and I'm going home now.'

'Oh, I'm in town, do you want to go to the Trafford Centre?'

So we went to Wetherspoons and had a nice long talk. It was really good. I thought, 'Ah, okay, she's clever,' and stuff like that, but I wasn't attracted in that way. She's not very tall and she used to dress in baggy clothes; but then one night we went out after one of these groups and she had this dress on, and she was *hot*.

I was like, 'What? Is this you? This is how you should dress, you know? This is really nice.'

And she said, 'Ah, thank you. It's the first time you've complimented me.'

We had fun that night. So we started hanging out.

We'd go to her mum's house as well. Her mum asked, 'How did you meet?'

Nat said, 'Oh, I just met her at this script-writing workshop.'

She had not come out to her parents. Her mum started asking questions, and Nat would try and shield me from them. But the thing is, she knew. They always know these things, don't they? Her mum knew even though she had not opened up to her.

Fast-forward to 1st January 2016. I was at this club called Lola's in the Northern Quarter. When Nat came, I said to her, 'Come and sit here!'

Everyone there knew me, and they were all saying, 'Is that the girl? Is that why you're not giving us all the attention?' and stuff like that.

Nat said, 'Oh, you're quite popular in the club,' and that just made her want to get me. By the end of the night we'd started kissing and she said, 'Please can you be my girlfriend?'

Now I was already liking her as well, but I still didn't know how to ask a girl or what to do. So I said, 'Oh, you've just made it easy!'

After I left Mark, I was staying with my friend John. Natalie was living with her nana, who didn't know anything about us. So when Nat said, 'I want to spend the night with you tonight,' we had to go round Manchester looking for a hotel. Unfortunately, we didn't get one. We went everywhere and didn't get anything. So we went back home…

When Natalie's grandad died she invited me to the funeral. So that was like my channel into the family, and then I gradually met them all. The nana just loved me. She'd say, 'Oh, I love Faith.' She'd say to me, 'Teach Natalie how to cook! Can you teach her this, can you teach her that?' She loved that African upbringing I have. They are of Caribbean heritage and she said I reminded her of herself when she was much younger. It's just that culture, the morals I have, that she'd teach Natalie. She used to tell me all these things. She died last year, unfortunately.

Claiming asylum

My visa had run out. I was not legal. Natalie said, 'You're too bright to live like this. We need to move on with our lives.' And to be fair, I was putting her life on pause as well. I didn't want that to happen, so that's what pushed me to claim asylum. And she's supported me through it, she's been amazing.

You have to go to a screening interview first, in Croydon. It was difficult, but luckily for me I had joined LISG, which really helped, because you get to know other people and become more confident. That really helped me. So I had some more confidence; and the lady who did my screening interview was very nice. I think she was lesbian as well. She did say to me, 'If I was the one granting you a stay, I would have given it to you.' So the screening interview was really good. The next interview was not. I felt the guy was poking too much, I felt like he didn't understand. Basically, the problem was, I got a man.

Unfortunately, we'd thought that my interview was going to be a video interview. I did get a letter saying it was. Everybody else had one-on-one, but the letter said, 'It's going to be a video interview; do not come with any evidence because there's no one to hand it over to.'

I checked with my solicitor. 'Should I go with the evidence, just in case?'

She said, 'No, no, I'm certain about it.'

I listened to her, but I should have taken it. As soon as I got there, I realised it was face-to-face.

They said, 'Have you got any evidence with you?'

I said 'No.' (I *should* have said, 'No, because I thought it was a video interview,' but I just said, 'No.')

So at the end, although I'd seen there was a question, 'Is there any further evidence to prove all of this?', he didn't even ask me that question, he just wrote 'No.'

And as soon as I saw that, I told my solicitor, 'We need to submit my evidence.'

They gave us five days, but she didn't submit it. The deadline was a Friday but she said, 'Oh, don't worry, I'll send it on Monday,' saying they shouldn't make any decision till they'd received it. There was no need for the delay because she had everything. I was a bit gutted, because they obviously made the decision on the fifth day – the letter was typed on the Friday – and that's because he was not expecting anything. So that was heartbreaking for me.

The Home Office refused me. I feel like it was because it

was a guy. When I got back, people were asking me, 'Why did you choose a guy?'

Yes, you can choose! You can say, 'I want a woman,' but I didn't know that.

So these are the things it is important for people to know. This guy did not understand my emotions. Again, maybe I'm not really good at expressing my feelings, so he could not understand certain things, but I still feel like, if it was a lady... Compare that to my first interview, my screening: she understood me, straight up. She was even finishing my sentences.

So, I've appealed against the decision, and this time they will have *all* my evidence. I couldn't have done this without Natalie, to be honest. I couldn't have. She's giving evidence as well. She's been my rock. I want to spend the rest of my life with Natalie. I have never felt the love and bond I feel with her with anyone else. I am a human who just wants to be happy with the woman I love. I tried to succumb to what my culture instils, but I have come to the realisation that I was born special and therefore I cannot and will not hide who I am. Lesbianism is not a phase – it is who I am.

~

Faith's appeal hearing was shortly after our interview, in March 2020. Immediately afterwards, the whole system closed down because of the Covid-19 pandemic. Under normal circumstances, it can take up to four weeks before the result of a hearing is known; but it was a long four months before, finally, the news came that Faith had been granted her refugee status. LISG members, still separated by the lockdown, shared their delight via WhatsApp. Faith is now continuing her education and training to build a career in IT.

KAREN M

The stories told so far show how utterly alone someone can feel, seeking asylum in this country, and what a difference can be made by kindness and practical support from others. This is why the work of a group like LISG is so important. From small beginnings in 2007, LISG has grown and developed so that there are currently some thirty members and half a dozen volunteers. These last three stories are told by women who have been involved with LISG since its very early days, and take us back in time to how it all began.

Karen M was involved in the formation of LISG and is still an enthusiastic advocate for the group. She started working with refugees in 2006, the year she turned fifty. Karen grew up in London at a time when lesbian lives were still very hidden and, like many of her generation, went out with boys until a political awakening to left-wing and feminist ideas in the 1980s led to her first relationship with a woman. She describes how events brought her to the Lesbian Community Project in Manchester, and how LISG grew out of their work.

I was born in South London on St Patrick's Day in 1956, to a Welsh mother and a Cornish father. My mum was a dancer; she met my dad when she was on tour and staying at the boarding house in Streatham run by his mum. I'm pretty certain Mum was pregnant when she got married – though she told me I was premature – so, as far as my paternal grandma was concerned, my mum was a scarlet woman. We moved out to Surrey when I was about seven, which my mum hated – she called it 'Toy Town'. I found it difficult to make friends at school. I seem to remember it being okay at my first school, but we moved in the first year of primary school, so presumably the other children had been at infants together, and all the girls already had a best friend. I remember it being quite painful.

One breaktime in the first year at secondary school, it

was raining, so we were indoors. There was mucking around going on and I was sat on my desk. I leapt off the desk and flung my arms around this girl, Susan, and gave her a big hug. And then I thought, 'Oh! They're all going to think I'm a lesbian!' Where did that come from? So somewhere very, very deep inside me was some self-knowledge, even at eleven or twelve. I also remember that in the sixth form I did have a fancy, a lust, for a student teacher. She was very peculiar looking – people would probably describe her as ugly. She was really small and quite underfed, with a strange face and a strange manner. And I just really fell for her, but I switched it off.

'Are you worried?'

My dad got cancer when I was fifteen and died around the time of my sixteenth birthday. I'd ended up being taken to the doctor's because I couldn't sleep. My mum had decided not to tell us about Dad's diagnosis, but she'd told a friend, and this friend took it upon herself to tell me that my dad had cancer. She told me because she thought my mum needed my support, but then swore me to secrecy! So that was very stressful. I'd come home and collapse onto my bed and sleep because I was exhausted, then hallucinate at night. So Mum took me to the doctor's.

Our lovely family doctor sat there and said to me, 'Are you worried about your dad?'

My mum was sat next to me so of course I said, 'No!'

Anyway, he put me on valium or something and I took my O levels. I got a respectable bunch of passes – though I was at a very good grammar school and I should probably have done a lot better.

After my dad died, my mum hit the ground running. She was in the middle of doing a nursery nursing course. She finished that; she came top of the class; she took us away on holiday. Then, in the autumn, she decided we were moving from Surrey up to London. She'd started drinking when my dad was ill and she became an alcoholic. I'm not sure where she was up to by the time we actually moved, because it took us all a while to fall in, or to admit what was happening. I was still a teenager and I travelled back down to Cheam in Surrey quite a lot of weekends to see my friends.

When I was about twelve or thirteen, I'd started going to the Girls' Brigade, and I joined the band, because we played the same night as the Boys' Brigade was on! I had a couple of boyfriends – in name and nothing else – and then I met this lad. We were boyfriend and girlfriend from when I was about fourteen. He had a very disruptive, dysfunctional home life, so I think he was probably ripe for getting involved in a relationship quite young; but why did I get so involved so young? I was with him before my dad was ill and we started having sex too. My mum worked that out and confronted me. I denied it, then admitted it, and she told me off, but I do remember feeling quite relieved, because she made me promise that I'd stop. And I did.

We started again after my dad had died, when I was sixteen, and got engaged. My mum threw a fit when she saw the ring on my finger. She didn't ban me from seeing him or anything, but she told me I was a silly little cow and if I thought I was going to marry him or move in with him, I had another think coming! But she didn't really deal with what it was about, which was that my dad had just died. Having got engaged to that lad, I split up with him that same summer. I fell in lust with somebody else, and I was with him, on and off, until I went away to uni three years later.

Political awakenings

I took a year out after school and worked in London. Then I went off to university. I hadn't been able to grieve for my dad. We didn't do grieving, we just carried on as usual; and there had been all the moving house and everything. I think I arrived at uni completely shut down emotionally. So I got involved with a young man very quickly and we limped through the next couple of years or so.

Then in my final year I got involved with this very beautiful young man who was in the year below me. I got to know some of his friends, and there were a couple of feminists. They took me off to a women's consciousness-raising group and... well! I've never been so terrified in my life. There were two *really* butch women there, and I'd never met butch women before and was absolutely terrified. So I only went that once. But the people I got to know around that young man were politically active, and that started to be my political awakening – feminism and other things. And I met my friend Mike, who was one of the founders of Lesbians and Gays Support the Miners. (I lost contact with him for years, and we reconnected only a couple of years ago. It was LGBT History Month and he was up here doing a talk, and I thought, 'That's got to be Mike!' That was lovely.)

So that was my political awakening.

Lesbian beginnings

Karen's boyfriend was working on his farm in Cornwall, so she rented a cottage there for Christmas, along with Mike and his boyfriend. They took her to meet a lesbian couple they knew.

I remember being *so* nervous beforehand, thinking, 'I'm going to meet these lesbians! What am I going to do if they fancy me? It's going to be terrible. I'll have to tell them I'm not...' That's what I remember going through in my head. So there I was in Cornwall with the lesbians. Nothing came of it, of course. They were lovely women. One of them worked for *Spare Rib* magazine.

I moved to London and started squatting with friends of my boyfriend – he eventually came to London too. I started doing bits of youth and community work, voluntary and part-time, and I had a summer job where I met a woman called Janet, who I thought was absolutely beautiful. I sort of fell for her, but I was still very involved with my boyfriend. Janet was out, which was slightly scary. We tinkered around at the edges, but nothing came of it. I did some volunteering for *Spare Rib*; my sister came and volunteered too.

We moved in these squatting circles doing bits and pieces of youth and community work, but I couldn't get a solid job, so I decided to get qualified. I came to Manchester because they had a course here, and also as a way of settling somewhere away from London that was near the mountains. I'd discovered mountaineering and was spending my few pennies – and all my time – on minibuses up and down to Wales and the Lakes. In London, I'd got involved in Red Rope, a socialist walking and climbing club, and in organising women-only trips (which didn't go down well with some of the men in the club). We also set up a group called Outdoor Women – the other women in that were lesbians. I moved to Manchester and a couple of them moved up this way too, to Hebden Bridge, so we started a group up here. Everybody else in that group, apart from me, was a lesbian!

My boyfriend got a job that meant he could move from London to Manchester. I remember I told him he'd have to organise his own social life, because all my friends were lesbians, so he wouldn't be able to socialise with my friends! And I used to say to people, 'Oh I'll probably have a relationship with a woman at some time.' So it's no surprise, really, that by the time he had moved up here he'd decided he didn't want to be with me any more. He ended up going back to London, to somebody he'd met down there. I was very upset – I was very attached to him. But then I went to the Alps with a friend from Red Rope and she brought a friend of hers, who I fell in lust with. She'd never had a relationship with a woman either, but we got it together on that trip. So that was it.

All this was in 1986, when I was thirty. And we were together for about three years, which was a mistake, but we were. Then she decided to have a relationship with a friend of mine – a good friend of mine, as I'd thought – and I didn't find out for eleven months. So that was all very painful, with all the brain-messing-about that goes on when something like that happens, all the deceit and stuff. Yeah. Then I had a rebound affair, and then I ended up on my own for about six or seven years.

At that point I did some serious therapy and started dealing with some of that stuff from much earlier. I think I'd done bits of counselling, but it was like sticking plaster, and this time I said to myself, 'If you're going to survive, actually you've got to sort it out.' So when I got to my fortieth birthday, for me it felt like a real celebration. I had a big party, because I'd seriously thought I wasn't going to get there, I'd been so depressed at times in my thirties.

So that's me, really, up to when I was forty. I went on to have two important lesbian relationships; and I've been single for about eleven years. I'm sixty-three now.

The beginning of LISG

I'd woken up a bit politically at uni and when I was squatting I volunteered for an advisory service for squatters. Then when I came to Manchester it was Clause 28. I'd been involved in setting up these women's outdoor groups, and I was doing youth and community work in a political way, but I always felt my politics was visceral, not rational. So I always felt a bit intimidated, for instance, by the SWP men in the mountaineering club, who could wipe the floor with you on all the theories.

But I got to a point in my life where I wasn't really doing anything much. I was in a relationship with a woman and we were quite cosy and domestic. Her dad had died, my mum had died, and it just felt like life had become very small and I had become very small. So I went to the Lesbian Community Project which then existed, which was at the Joyce Leyland Centre. I went to Lisa, who was one of the workers there; it was the only project in the country that was funded to work with lesbians. Now, I do not to this day know where this came from, but I said I wanted to do some volunteering and was particularly interested in immigration. Something I'd absorbed, somewhere – I don't know where. I didn't even know there was an issue around sexuality and immigration! But it lit something in me.

At that time, a woman called Florence had contacted them and asked for help with her campaign. She was from Sierra Leone; she had a son, she'd been refused, she'd gone to court representing herself. A very steep learning curve for me! I met Florence, we chatted a bit, and I began to do things with her. That was in the autumn of 2006. In 2007, I organised a meeting at the centre for anybody who was interested, and Karen S came to that, and quite a few others.

In April 2007, we organised a women's bop as a fund-raiser for Florence's campaign. There hadn't been one for a long time (women's things were sort of disappearing), so it was really busy. We raised over a thousand pounds, we raised the profile, and we all had a great night. Florence was bowled over by the size of the event and the sense of support. She'd never seen anything like it, and all focussed on her!

'A steep learning curve'

We'd taken a collection tin around the gay village, and Lisa had contacted the bars saying, 'Can we come and collect?' Florence came, with some of her friends from Women Asylum Seekers Together, including a wheelchair user and three straight women. Some of us went round the bars and that was a steep learning curve. The number of people

– LGBT people – who said, 'What's it got to do with us? Why do you believe her? She's probably lying!' Or, 'It's not our fault she was born somewhere like that, it's nothing to do with us.' That sort of stuff. The place that was best was a bar where it tends to be older men, dressed in their leathers and all that, but who'd been involved in gay rights. And they got it. They absolutely got it. Some of the bars that had given permission on the phone for us to collect, changed their minds, because they didn't want their customers upset, they wanted them to have a nice time. It's not like that now. In terms of the LGBT community, it's so much more out there that this is an issue. Some of the women in LISG joined the Lesbian and Gay Chorus, and for a long time it was just one or two women there who said, 'We need to do something to support these people.' The others were not making the connection, but they eventually got it.

After Florence got her status – through the government legacy scheme applied to longstanding cases – she said to us, very clearly, 'I wouldn't have lasted this long in my campaign without you and your support.' Overlapping that, there was Prossy, whose campaign was being spearheaded by the Metropolitan Community Church and we gave some support to that. And we thought, 'Well, that's two – there must be more.' That's when we formed LISG. So that would have been sometime late in 2007. But we count it, really, from Florence's campaign starting, so it's thirteen years this month. We went from being a biggish group to a quite small group, though. A couple of the women who we supported early on became involved as LISG volunteers.

Over the years, we've been contacted by other people saying, 'Oh, we'd like to do this, that and the other,' but that can also mean more work for us. It often came down to just two or three of us, and not having the wherewithal.

I withdrew from LISG in the autumn before last, because I had major surgery and thought I hadn't got it in me to be supporting other people. I'm assuming the way it works is still the same. Some things have changed, though! We used to go to Pride and they'd say, 'Lesbian Immigration Support? What's that about?' But *now* it's: 'Lesbian Immigration Support? Woah!' And they'll be cheering! It makes me cry, because it's such a big difference over the years.

PROSSY

Prossy fled to the UK from Uganda in 2007 and – as Karen M described – was one of the first women to be supported by LISG. After she was granted refugee status, Prossy became a volunteer in her turn. Now she is using her own experience of the process to help other refugees and people seeking asylum. Prossy's story contains episodes of physical torture and of terrible mental suffering; but it is also, as are so many of the stories in this book, an illustration of extraordinary determination and courage in the face of persecution.

My mum's an amazing woman. She was a wonderful mother to me and I had a brilliant childhood. When I was about thirteen, I found out she wasn't my biological mother. I was the product of an affair and I was brought home to my mum because my biological mother passed away. It was a middle-class upbringing; we had a country house and a city house, but we spent most of the time in the city. My dad didn't believe a lot in educating girls, but my mum was an assertive woman who fought very hard for me to get a great education and to go to good schools, the same as my brothers did. I had a huge family, lots of cousins, so in the holidays we would all go to the village, to the country house. Everyone had chores to do. You might be assigned a place to do the gardening: 'You must do from here to there!' (Which turned me off gardening for life, because I hated it. I'm not the most green-fingered of people.)

But I had a great childhood, and I loved school. I loved it, because my father was a very strict person. You would be having fun, but as soon as he came home, everything stopped. He wouldn't tolerate anything and he did beat us. So, I loved boarding school. I went from the age of seven. I loved being with other kids and away from home, until a certain age. After I reached my teens and became aware of myself and my sexuality, I stopped enjoying school as much as I did before.

'I liked the look of the girls'

I discovered my attraction to girls at about fourteen, when the other girls were getting interested in boys and talking about the boys they liked, and I didn't have that compulsion. I didn't feel anything for any of the boys. I liked the look of the girls. I didn't fit in, in that way. The older we got, the more I became aware of my sexuality, that I genuinely did like girls. Because of what I saw happening outside and to LGBT people around us, I was scared. I knew about all that: the preachings in church, especially. I went to a Catholic school and they are very voluble about certain things, and the preachings were very... almost fixated, sometimes, on sexuality, and what happens to people 'like that'. It started to happen around us, that people got killed because of their sexuality. Of course, because I was interested in it, I also became interested in the law. So I knew that in Uganda it was punishable by prison; you go to prison. It's immoral... and I started self-hating, and thinking that I wasn't normal, whatever 'normal' is. That was when my love for school started dwindling a little bit.

I was born in '81, so this would be around the mid 90s. Back then, it wasn't as much spoken about as it became later on, at the beginning of the 2000s. But I think if you are like that yourself, then you tend to listen out for it more, and you pay more attention to what's going on. The older I got, the worse it got; I think because people became braver about talking about who they are and what they are. The more people came out about it – and even the more it happened in the west – the more it got noticed in countries like Uganda and the more people talked about it. 'You see what's happening in that country? It's crazy, they're going mad! They've just agreed for these people to have rights!' and so on. So it had repercussions. I liked girls, I admired them from afar, and I would have my imaginary situations in my own mind, but I was too scared to have a relationship at school.

'The most amazing time'

When you get to university, on one hand you have more bravado and more open-minded people, but then there is the opposite, the ones who are more conservative, saying, 'I think it's disgusting!' You have the liberal voices, too, who say, 'They can do what they want! People can do whatever!' University was where I met Leah. We got drunk one day – it was all the product of alcohol! – and one thing led to another. That's how it all started. Then I got to learn more about the underground places you could go to, where all the other similar people are, so you could hang out. University opened my eyes and my life to a whole different world that I never knew existed. It was scary, but at the same time it was most liberating, and I think I had the most amazing time of my life. Experimenting and seeing all these different people, going to places where it was completely underground, but you could see people living their best life – it was amazing. It was completely amazing.

Leah and I started a relationship, but we were known as 'best friends'. She could come to my house, I could go to her house, and our parents knew each other. When they came to see us at university, they met, and so on.

After I finished university, I started working with my mum: she had a chain of shops selling second-hand clothes. Jobs are not easy to find straight away after you've finished uni.

But my father thought it was a good time for me to get married. He said, 'Either you find your own husband, or I'll find you one.'

Obviously, I wasn't going to find one!

My mum tried to say, 'She's still young, she can do her own thing.'

My father got the son of one of his business mates to marry me. And it was just the most awful time. It was awful for me and Leah both. My father said I was old enough to marry, and obviously it made business sense for the families to join. This fellow had no choice. There was absolutely no choice, and we had the traditional ceremony of introduction.

'They found us'

Leah said, 'I can't come to see this.' But after the ceremony she came to visit me. At that time, I wasn't sleeping in the main house. It's a big compound: we have a main house and then other little houses which are supposed to be maids' quarters, but all the children can sleep there and be at home but have privacy as well. So I had one of those. Leah came and one thing led to another...

But we were not safe. We did not protect ourselves. My brother and my fiancé found us. They found us and they took us to the police station themselves. My brother and my fiancé, they took us. We gathered a little crowd, it made the local news, and it was horrendous. We were both put in prison. That was the last time I saw Leah for a number of years.

I was in prison for two weeks. That isn't long, but it was the longest time of my life. In prison, if they know why you're there, they treat you worse than a murderer. There's a culture of, 'You're like that because you haven't met a real man,' and they know that whatever happens, nobody's going to pay much attention to it. So... a lot of things happened in there. It was a horrendous fortnight that's still haunting me to this day. You learn to live with the scars but they never go away. I had physical scars, because they enjoyed the torture; they burned me really badly, all over my legs... But it's the mental scars that remained from my sexual assault that hurt more than the physical ones.

Uganda is corrupt and my family bought me out. My dad paid for me to be freed and I thought, 'Oh, this is great!'

But it wasn't, because then it crossed over from the legal realm to the realm of witchcraft. They were saying, 'This is a curse that's going to go to the whole family. It's going to catch all the other members of the family!'

I don't know if I'll ever forget that day when they collected me. My dad came with my brother, they collected me, and I think they knew what had happened to me in there. No, I don't *think* they knew – I *know* they knew. I don't think they cared that much. Because I hadn't bathed, I stank (and some of that stink, I can still smell it sometimes). They knew.

We went to the village, to the house, and they were going to do something. They brought bark-cloth that they use for traditional ceremonies, and there were some beads and stuff. I don't know if it was going to be an exorcism, or what it was going to be, but I knew I was not safe there. I had no way out. And I was there for days.

'Just get away!'

I knew they were waiting for someone – I think it was someone who was going to do this ceremony. The day came and my dad went to collect this person, and my mum helped me to escape. It's one of those things that always makes me cry when I talk about it. I love that woman so much and I don't think I would be alive if it wasn't for her. I don't think I would be. But she helped me escape. She had drained her business and she had all this plan arranged for me. She gave me a bag and it was full of money, and a passport, and she said, 'Just run! Just run and go!' She told me the name of a village and said, 'There is an agency there. Just go away, anywhere. Go to Kenya. Anywhere you can go, just get away, because this is not good.' And that's how I got away.

I was walking for a long time. I don't even know how long it was. Then I saw a car and I said to the driver, 'I'll give you a lot of money to take me to this and this place.' And they took me. I went to that agency and they said, 'We would have taken you through Entebbe, but we can't go there now.' Because by that time my name was everywhere. If it's a case of corruption, the only way they can justify you being out of prison is by saying you escaped: so then your name is put out as an escapee. I had to leave Uganda, but I couldn't go through the airport because I was an escapee from prison and they would have caught me, so I went through Kenya.

At first my destination was Canada, but that fell through. He said, 'We can't use your passport,' so I had to get rid of my passport. And then because I didn't have a visa and we were not going to go through the right channels, they did this thing where they change the photo – everything else in the passport is genuine, apart from the photo. So it becomes your photo, but in a passport with a visa and a different name. That agency, they get visas for people. And my first was Canada, but the Canada one fell through, then it was Sweden, and that one fell through as well, and the UK was actually my third choice.

I was going to wear a dress, because the burns on my legs had become boils and they were horrendously painful, but he said, 'You can't wear a dress. They don't wear dresses there.'

Someone said, 'It's July, she can wear a dress.'

But he said, 'No, that would be too suspicious. She would just look like an African village woman, whereas if she wears jeans, she will look more sophisticated.'

I'll never forget that! I was thinking, *'Trousers* make you *sophisticated*? Who knew?' So I wore jeans, with my boils on my legs, and it was just horrible. Horrible.

We got on the plane, and – it felt like I just blinked and we were there, but at the same time, it felt like ages. Like forever and ever. When we arrived at Heathrow, we came out together, walked out, and I was scared shitless because I knew this wasn't my passport. But we passed through and came out, and the man from the agency gave me an address. He said, 'That's where you should go to get help.' And he took the passport from me and said, 'But from here on in, you're on your own.'

I had nothing. I had a few clothes and some money in pounds – I think it was twenty-five pounds or something – and that bought me a ticket to Croydon, to the Home Office. He'd given me the information I needed, which was super, and I went from Heathrow to Croydon that same day.

I arrived in Croydon and they took my details. Of course, the man who had helped me didn't know why I was running away. He had read snippets in the papers about me, but it wasn't something we talked about.

He had told me, 'This is the place you go to ask for help.' But I didn't know what to expect at all. He said, 'Just be honest with them.'

'They did apologise, later'

So I went there and, actually, I passed out, because I hadn't eaten for a very long time and I was in all this pain and everything.

They asked me, 'Why are you here?'

And I said, 'Because I'm running away, because I was in prison.'

I was scared because I had never, ever, in my life gone up to someone and said, 'I am gay.' And it was just at an open window and there's a lot of people sat behind you. It's awful.

That interview was the strangest experience of my entire life. I didn't know what to do, I didn't know what to say, I didn't know anything. I think I speak good English but they got an interpreter for me, from Uganda, and on the side she was saying to me, 'It's people like you who give

Uganda a bad name. We do not have this type of people in our country. You're giving our country a bad name.'

If it was now, I would be saying, 'Shut down the interview!' but back then I didn't know if she was a person in power. Was she going to decide my case? Was she the person who was supposed to help me? She was horrible! (Later on, I wished I had caught her name, because I would have put in a complaint. I tried to find out, but I never could.)

Later, I found out that the only reason I didn't go straight into detention was because it was full; there was no space. So they put me in a bed and breakfast, because it was late, and the following day we got in a van and came to Bolton.When I arrived in Bolton they put me in temporary accommodation. I was in so much pain, and there was a girl who said to me, 'You know you can go to hospital if it's an emergency? You can register with a GP, but there's a walk-in centre in Bolton.'

I went to this walk-in centre and they asked what was the problem, and I showed them my legs. The nurse was so shocked. She said, 'I'll be back in a minute.' She went away and she called the police.

I was scared because I'd been tortured at the hands of the police. But the policewoman said, 'We just want to help. Nothing is going to happen, we're just going to help. What's happened to you?'

And I just said, 'I have pain on my legs.' I couldn't say the other stuff.

She said, 'You can talk to me.'

She was nice and I did tell her some bits of my story – not all of it, but I think she surmised what had happened.

Then she said, 'Okay, we can't treat you here, but we're going to take you to a place that's specialist.' So the police took me to St Mary's, the rape referral centre here in Manchester.

Now, they did apologise to me later. However, knowing what I had just told them, they made me get into a police van with two police *men*! It was really horrendous. I developed claustrophobia in that police van. I just wanted to get out and it was really, really horrible. But they were nice, they did apologise to me later on.

We went to St Mary's rape referral centre and the police took the forensic photos, and St Mary's wrote a detailed report. It hadn't been long since everything had happened so they could still get the evidence they needed, which was good for me and for my case. But it was *so* hard! The intrusive testing – I know they had to, but the intrusive tests – I felt like I wasn't given a choice of 'Do you want us to do this?' It's difficult to think about things in terms of your case, but I have to. It was great for my case later on, because I had that evidence of torture and everything.

When we were leaving, the policemen were so lovely, bless them. I think they really did notice that I was uncomfortable around them, and then they started chatting to me: 'What do you like?'

I said, 'I like football.'

So when we were driving back, they passed by Manchester United's ground and we stopped outside, which was lovely. So they were sweet and they did try, but it would have been helpful not to have had to go through all that.

Later on, they sent someone to my house to do the forensic photos and again they sent a man. They did! I said no. I think he himself realised as well. He said, 'We'll come back later and a woman will come.' She said what had happened was a mess-up. But they were nice. This was in 2007.

Campaigning

And that's when my battle with the Home Office started. I got refused! I thought it was going to be straightforward, because I obviously had the hospital evidence, the forensic photos of the torture, a clipping from the newspaper with me being arrested and all that.

They said, 'Yes, we agree that she's been attacked, but it was an attack by random police officers and not targeted at her specifically. She can go back and relocate to another part of the country.' This was when the Home Office still had the relocation strategy. Yeah. 'She can go back and relocate.'

I had a really awful solicitor at the time; I think they messed up my case a bit. Then I had to go to court and my solicitor messed up so badly that she wrote a skeleton argument saying I was from Azerbaijan. I had never heard of a country called Azerbaijan at that time. She gave me this skeleton argument to sign and I did sign it. When I read, 'She can't be returned to Azerbaijan,' I was thinking, 'Gosh, I thought my English was good, but this is amazing, it must be another word for persecution!' So we took this document to court and the judge said, 'I thought your client was from Uganda?' We were thrown out of court, the hearing didn't go ahead, because everything was so clearly a copy-and-paste job.

There's an LGBT church in Manchester, the Metropolitan Church. The minister there pointed me to Greater Manchester Immigration Aid Unit (GMIAU) and they gave me a solicitor. I was losing the will to live at the time, because my old solicitor was so crap and was refusing to give me my file. But this GMIAU solicitor called her: 'Listen. You owe this woman an apology for messing up her case and saying she's from a different country, and you have to give me that file *now*! If you don't give me that file...'

And I was like, 'Yes, woman! Go on!' I think I got hope, then. That's when I started getting hope. After that, my case was passed on to another solicitor at GMIAU. She was great. Sometimes she stayed until 10pm, taking statements from my supporters.

Then of course, at the time I started my fight, I got into campaigning. Because the Metropolitan Church was promoting this: 'You can do a campaign and talk about your case.' I went to Pride, I talked on the stage, went to

Brighton Pride. I was collecting signatures. It was then that I met Karen and other women who were helping at LISG. I met both the Karens (Karen M and Karen S) when they were doing the Florence campaign. Florence and I were seeking asylum at the same time and I started going to the campaign for her.

After Florence got her status, they decided we needed to continue this kind of work and I was one of the first other persons they started helping. They were so, so supportive. They went to court with me and to different places to get signatures. They stood on the street in the gay village and asked people, 'Can you add your signature? She's a lesbian from Uganda.'

Just as Karen M had seen with Florence, there was resistance to Prossy's petition.

You would be surprised at how many people in the gay village refused to sign it. They would say, 'No, go back to your country,' or, 'If people like you leave your countries, then who's going to change things? You have to stay there and fight for your own rights, like we did here.' Men, mostly.

Karen S walked Canal Street with me, looking for signatures from people and explaining to them. She is the most amazing woman I've met, apart from my mother. She just has the biggest heart. Yeah. I could cry talking about her. She's been my sister and my confidante, and when I feel low, when I'm happy, when I'm everything in between, she's there. I'm just the most blessed person to have her. And I met her at a time when I was really, really the most down, even if I didn't know it at the time.

'I didn't look lesbian enough'

My campaign gained momentum and I went to court again, but I was again refused. And do you know why? I love a lipstick, as you can tell. I love makeup, I love high heels. They said, 'She came to court and she did not look like a lesbian.' I was actually refused on those terms, because I didn't look lesbian enough! So again, I continued campaigning and I still had another appeal left. I appealed and I got my status that time. I look back now and think, 'You were one of the lucky ones,' because all this happened so quickly. Within a year, I had my status, and these days people wait so much longer. Even then, some people waited so much longer. But at the time, I felt like it was going on forever.

But after I got my status, I had to face things, you know. What you've been through, you have to face it. So hard. So, so hard. I got in touch with my mum and she said, 'I love you and I'm glad you're safe, but don't contact me again.' I think she wanted it for her own safety, and that hurt. It hurt so bad. And that was the first time that I did try to take my life. When I did that, I was sectioned. I was in hospital, and Karen visited me all the time. She brought me potato and leek soup. Well, it was the first time I'd ever heard of anything like that. I was saying, 'Karen? You took *perfectly good potatoes* and you decided to mash them up like baby food?' I'd never heard of this soup culture! We still laugh about it. I do love her soup now, but at the time I couldn't eat it. Why anyone would take nice potatoes and mash them up to make them like baby goo... But yeah, she came and saw me in hospital all the time when I was there. I was there for months, actually.

After I left hospital, it was a difficult road to recovery. Even after I got my status, I was still in and out of the psychiatric ward and still suicidal. So it took time to get back on my feet. But I was volunteering with LISG from the start. I couldn't do casework, because for me it was a trigger, but I could do other things. And for the other women, it helped them to see an almost-success story, someone who's been through it and come out the other end.

'Family reunion'

After I settled down and got a little flat and started working, Leah was my drive. She was like a focus for me, so it was a blessing in disguise. I didn't know where she was and I spent quite a lot of money asking. I contacted Leah's sister, who took a stupid amount of money from me under the guise of looking for Leah, and I later found out that she wasn't doing anything. I have one really amazing friend in Uganda who kept in touch. I couldn't contact her before, because I was scared of getting in touch with anyone. I got in touch with this friend, she helped me, and we tracked Leah down in a prison in the northern part of Uganda, miles and miles and miles away, four years later. Again, because of corruption, it would be possible to buy her out. So I worked my ass off (pardon my French) and I did it. Four years after I got here, early in 2011, I managed to get her out by paying. I saw her for the first time in a video call! Then I got her a place to stay and was supporting her; and then, a year later, I did a 'family reunion'.

When you get your refugee status, under the Human Rights Convention you're entitled to apply for your family members to join you. It was a struggle – of course it wasn't going to be straightforward – because they asked for a marriage certificate. I said, 'We come from Uganda! How were we going to get married?' And I appealed. I had to pay for a solicitor at one point, who didn't help much, but again the Immigration Aid Unit came to the rescue. That's why I always campaign for them and I'm a donor now for life. Ryan put in a lot of hours to help me and Leah, and we did a successful family reunion application. And she came. She never even went through the asylum process, because when they join you, they take your status. So I applied for her to join me as my partner, and she already came with the refugee status, the jammy cow! She came here in May 2014 and she's here now.

Working life

I work with the British Red Cross now. After I arrived here, I went to different charities for help as a refugee and I loved the support, the sort of things you could do for someone who has just arrived when they don't have any hope. So I knew I wanted to work with people in that way. There was one group run by the British Red Cross, working with refugee women in Bolton, which I accessed as a service user. Then, when I got my status, the person who was running it left. (Her name is Anna and she's still a good friend of mine. When I was trying to raise money to bring Leah, she did a walk and collected money for me. I'm surrounded by amazing women, I really am. I'm so blessed.) So I applied to run that women's group and I got the job! I was running that for two years. After that, the funding changed, I still stayed, and now I run hubs in Bolton and Leigh for refugees and asylum seekers.

I run one of our biggest hubs in Bolton: I can get maybe a hundred and twenty people in one day. It's for refugees who have just arrived in the area. It's a social drop-in with immigration advice and simple things like how to apply for a GP, how to get to the library, the things you're entitled to, where to get English classes. From simple things like that, to: 'I don't have a solicitor; I need to put in my fresh claim; can you help me to bring my family?' I love it, love it, love it! So, I work with refugees and asylum seekers, and I enjoy it so much.

Leah is a support worker. She's more outgoing than I am, so she liked coming to the gay village, whereas I'm over it! I say, 'You go, I'll pick you up.' She likes to go out and have a good time. It wasn't easy, getting back into our life together, because we were separated for so long. Before, she was the 'out there' one, and when she came here the roles were reversed: I was the confident one and she'd been in prison for four years. But we lived to tell the tale. And we're thankful every day. Sometimes it's not so easy, because some things that you've been through, they live with you forever. They don't go away, do they? You just learn how to live with it and how to cope.

KAREN S

I interviewed Karen S on 29 January 2020. As we were talking, she realised that it was the anniversary of the meeting in 2007 from which the Lesbian Immigration Support Group eventually grew. Karen has volunteered with the group for the whole of those thirteen years, and has become a key figure in its continuing success.

She was born in 1961 in Scarborough, a seaside resort in North Yorkshire, and lived there till she was twenty-one. Her father was a poultry dealer and her mother had been a sewing machinist before marrying. Karen described her childhood as fairly unremarkable – until she discovered feminism, which was to shape the rest of her life.

I think *The Women's Room* was the first feminist book I read, and that started a bit of an awakening. It was just about reading and thinking; I wasn't actually aware of any women's groups. Around that time, I started getting interested in environmental issues as well. I remember joining Friends of the Earth. There wasn't anything local in Scarborough, so I was chatting with the office in London, saying 'How do you set up a group?' I started talking to people locally, like at the wholefood shop, trying to set up a local Friends of the Earth group. And that happened. So, I started doing little actions. My sister who I'm close to (she's two years older) was into environmental stuff as well, and probably started getting involved in feminism to some degree. But my parents? I can't remember them even mentioning it. When I became vegetarian, it was like, 'Oh, it's just a phase!' They basically pooh-poohed it. So, I was in my late teens when I started getting involved in politics. My parents were dyed-in-the-wool Tories, so it was quite a lot to rebel against!

I left school when I was seventeen, about halfway through my A levels. I'd got quite interested in alcohol! After that I did odd jobs. I spent a lot of my youth on the dole and getting involved in politics. I think at that time it was much easier to do that, and quite common in lesbian and feminist politics: you did your activism and you could be on the dole. It's a completely different landscape today. In Scarborough there was seasonal work, so I was a chambermaid in a hotel for a couple of seasons. And then, at that time, there was the Youth Opportunity Programme. I remember looking at this list of opportunities and the only one that interested me was working in the parks department. So I said, 'I'd like a job as a gardener.'

'I wouldn't back down'

I had to fight to get taken on; they tried very hard to put me off. It was, 'Oh, we don't really take women in the gardens.' I remember going to the interview and being told, 'You know, it's hard work. You've got to wear steel toe-cap boots. There's only one toilet...'

But I wouldn't back down. I was adamant. I said, 'No, this is what I want to do.'

Then, grudgingly, they took me on as a youth placement, working at the council nursery for the gardens.

Now, generally, after four to six weeks, the men that they took on, if they were half decent, they'd get taken on temporary. I'd been on twice as long as that, and I was more than half decent compared to them. I've always been a bit of a grafter, but I had to fight to do things. I remember once, this lorry came in and there were bags of compost. They were unloading the lorry and I was told to go off and do something else. I was like, 'Come on! Don't wrap me in cotton wool!' And I proved that I could do the job. Finally, grudgingly, they did take me on temporary and I worked a couple of seasons in the parks. I was fly-mowing these banks up by the cliffs one day, in the park, and I remember one couple looking from the bottom of the bank where I had this fly-mower on a rope, looking up at me, and asking, 'Are you a man or a woman?' So even going to work was activism of a kind, because I had to fight for it! When I think back, because I was the only woman there, I got a lot of harassment, including sexual harassment. I did raise my voice against it, but not half as much as I would if it happened now. Different times.

I did that for a couple of years in the season and got laid off in the winter. By the time I was about twenty, I was saying, 'I want to be taken on permanent' – because all the blokes were. I was very blatantly told that the only way they'd take me on permanent, because I was a woman, was if I was redeployed to the grounds of the crematorium. And when the person who burned the bodies was away on holiday, I'd have to do that job. So I thought, 'Sod that for a game of soldiers!' I was wanting to leave Scarborough anyway. It was a small-town atmosphere: very nice in a lot of ways, but, you know, the nearest city is York, which is sixty miles away, and York's not the most cosmopolitan place.

I was involved in Friends of the Earth, getting their co-ordinators' newsletters every month, and I noticed the Lewisham branch was setting up a loft insulation and draught-proofing scheme for the homes of elderly people. So I applied for a job with the scheme as a loft insulator. It was a long way away but it felt exciting. And I was ready for it: as I say, that small-town atmosphere of Scarborough... I'd been to a couple of local group conferences in London and met various people, so I went and stayed for a while with someone I'd met in London, and got the job.

'They were all lesbians'

At this point I wasn't out. I didn't come out till I was twenty-three. It was interesting, actually, on the loft insulating project: of those of us who went out and did the work, there were three or four women, and the supervisor was a woman as well. And there were three blokes. We could wipe the floor with them. I learned so much from the other women… I was going to say carpentry skills, but that wasn't all! I didn't know they were all lesbians; that was something I was completely unaware of at the beginning. Over the course of the year that the project ran, I got very close to one of them and ended up having a bit of a relationship, a bit of a fling. I was always like, 'I don't know what's happening, this isn't me.' Little did I know! But that was the start of that sort of awakening.

When I did come out, a couple of years after that, and then looked back on my childhood, it was just so obvious that I was *always* a lesbian! I had a massive crush on a best friend at school and we used to kiss. I remember a couple of other kids in the class looking at me and being like, 'Oh, you like So-and-so!' and me thinking, 'My God, they think I'm a lesbian.' But I had no inkling at that time – even though I was in love with my best friend – no inkling that I might be a lesbian. I suppose because lesbians were these horrible, disgusting women, and that wasn't me, so I didn't make that connection and absolutely pushed that down. So when it happened, it was, 'Oh, what's happening? This isn't me!' It took me by surprise. Then when I did come out, when I was twenty-three, I started remembering and it was a complete revelation.

So it all started that year, with having a fling with this woman. I had a couple of boyfriends after that, for the next couple of years. I became vegetarian when I was still in Scarborough, and vegan when I was twenty-one and got involved in animal rights. I met quite a lot of people through meetings. I was living in a bedsit in South London, and I met a lot of people in North London who were squatting in the Wood Green and Tottenham area.

I felt a bit isolated where I was, so I ended up moving into a squat with them. I got involved in a bit of activism; a lot of them were anarchists, so I got interested and joined a local anarchist group. I look back on that time with real fondness. It was 1982 when I moved to London and I came out in 1984. It was a very political time – there was so much happening. And, as I say, you could be on the dole: I spent most of my twenties on the dole. I thought that that's how it would always be. I had no concept of wanting paid work, I just wanted to be a political activist all my life. So, heady times.

Getting involved in anarchist politics increased my social circle. There were quite a lot of women in our group and I started getting involved in various women's stuff, like campaigning against pornography and going to demos at Greenham Common. Around that time there was a women's hospital in Clapham that the government closed, and it was occupied by the staff. All the medical staff were women, the staff occupied the hospital, then activists got involved as well. I used to go down there a couple of days a week and we used to sleep over on the wards. So that was exciting, sitting in all these chairs around this big room, having these big collective meetings and talking about what to do when the police evicted us, making plans – and we used to have socials there. That was round about the time I'd just come out. Very exciting.

New directions

I was in London till I was twenty-five and then I went to Sheffield for a couple of years, which seemed very boring compared to London. It seemed small. So I went back. On my second stint in London, a friend asked me if I fancied going to an evening class to learn sign language, so I went along. My friend dropped out after a few weeks but I got hooked, and at the end of that class I'd got level one BSL. Then the tutor told us there was a one-year funded course we could do, specifically to work with further education, with deaf students. So I did that. I thought it was a great opportunity to learn all these skills: sign language, note-taking and lipspeaking skills.

Then I decided I wanted to come back up north. I came to Manchester and I've been in this area ever since. It was becoming more difficult to be on the dole at that time, so I set up as self-employed. I did college support work with deaf students, then went on to do further courses and an interpreting degree for BSL/English. I did interpreting for about ten years, then I got a bit bored and retrained as a hearing therapist. Within the first year or so, I realised counselling was a big part of that job, so I did NVQ level three in counselling skills. I didn't go on further because I was happy as a hearing therapist in the NHS, though the atmosphere could be difficult at times.

After seventeen years, I felt I needed to leave. I knew there wasn't the possibility of getting a job as a hearing therapist somewhere else, because there were so few posts, so I was at the stage of, 'Well, what can I do? I'm in my late fifties!' This plan seemed to hatch and I started getting excited about retraining as a counsellor, and going back to studying. Because I'd never been down that route: I'd got a BSL/English interpreting degree, but I was working part-time when I did it. As I said, I'd left school at seventeen. I'd gone to night school and got A levels, but the thought of being a real student, that was quite exciting. You never know where life's going to take you.

It was 1990 when I moved to Manchester. I started meeting people and, for a few years, I was involved in the Troops Out movement. The Manchester branch was virtually all women and probably about half of us were lesbians. I was on the mailing list for the Lesbian Community Project and one day I got an email from Lisa, the co-ordinator, saying a woman from Sierra Leone had come into the LCP wanting to know if she could get any support.

How LISG began

That woman was Florence and – like Karen M – Karen S recalls the meeting that would lead to the founding of LISG.

I think at that time it was quite difficult for lesbians to access mainstream asylum groups: Florence didn't feel able to be out and let other asylum seekers know why she was claiming.

So this email came, saying, 'Is anyone interested in getting together and setting up an anti-deportation campaign?' and I said I was interested. Then, on 29th January 2007 – thirteen years ago today – we had that very first meeting. There was maybe a dozen of us. I can't remember any of us knowing anything about asylum, but we were interested in doing something and getting involved. Florence was there; I can't remember if her son Michael was – he was probably about four at the time. At that meeting, we decided to set up an anti-deportation campaign. And that was it, really. It was a steep learning curve, learning about the asylum process and trying to raise the profile.

After about a year, Florence got her leave to remain; but other lesbians who were seeking asylum started to gravitate towards the group. I can remember at least three who got in touch during the campaign, and a couple who came to some of the meetings because it was a safe place to be, and they wanted support as well. The first time I met Prossy was at the celebration of Florence getting her stay; I then got involved in Prossy's campaign. So we were starting to be aware there was a need here. We'd gained skills and knowledge over that year, so we thought, 'We need to carry on.' We just became the Lesbian Immigration Support Group! Karen M, Lisa from LCP and me took it on, growing from those very early days. We used to have monthly meetings – about six or eight of us sat around with four or five women who were going through the system – and we got more knowledge, more confidence.

I suppose we were finding out what we could do that was different from other support groups. There were other groups that people dipped into, like Women Asylum Seekers Together in Manchester – even now, quite a few of our members will be in WAST as well as in LISG. You know, women always talk about 'family' when they talk about LISG. That word comes up so often. I think the fact that it's all women is its real strength: it's a safe place, and the vast majority of LISG members have gone through sexual violence at one level or another. It's that safe space to come together, where we're all women, and it's a place where women can feel safe and tell their stories if they want to. Also it's helpful because, well, how do you prove your sexuality?

The process

The Home Office is so hit-and-miss. With some women I'll think, 'Oh yes, she'll get her stay easily, comparatively speaking,' because some are more 'obvious' to the Home Office. That is to say, from a western perspective they'd look like a more stereotypical lesbian. So as we went along, it's almost as if we had to become 'expert lesbians'! The Home Office wants 'proof' of someone's sexuality, so we have to ask ourselves, 'Why do we believe this woman is a lesbian?' and then actually try to put it into words – to make the implicit, explicit.

Because all the volunteers are lesbian and bisexual women, and that's always been the case, it's about bringing in a part of yourself as well. When I came out in 1984, I had that realisation that I'm a lesbian, but before that I had to push it down. When I was born, male homosexuality was still illegal in the UK. In the 80s, there was political awareness and there was Section 28, and you had the experience of people shouting 'Dyke!' at you on the street, and stuff like that – though that's nothing compared to what

LISG members have been through. Also, I had relationships with blokes in my late teens and early twenties, whereas if I had realised being a lesbian had been a possibility, I would have embraced it earlier. So many LISG members have had forced marriages, or thought they were heterosexual because it wasn't on their radar that there was any other possibility. So, giving evidence in Grace's case, for instance, with the Home Office saying, 'Why didn't she do this?' or 'Why did she do that?' in 1980s Uganda, I could say, 'Actually, this is my experience in the UK in the 1980s, so I can understand why she felt that she needed to do that.' It's just trying to make them understand that there's nothing unusual in why a lesbian did this, or didn't do that, in the circumstances she's in at the time.

'Always firefighting'

At the moment, we've probably got about thirty to thirty-five members. Of the volunteers, currently two of us are established and experienced, and four or five are newer volunteers who are starting to get more established. We're an unincorporated charitable organisation. We did try and go down the charity route a few years ago, but it took up so much time, and we're always firefighting; for instance, if someone gets detained... So it kind of fell by the wayside.

We had to set the geographical limit of Greater Manchester: you have to be living in the area to get support from LISG. Over the years, we've got a higher profile, more people know about us, and we get emails from all over the world. We get these really heart-wrenching emails, like, 'I'm in Uganda, I'm in Egypt, I'm in Pakistan, this is my situation – can you help me?' Dire situations. 'Me and my girlfriend just want to escape, can you tell me how?' It's awful. We just have to write back, wish them well, and say, 'If you do get out, claim asylum straight away, because if you don't claim it at the port it will be held against you; and we can only help you if you're in the Manchester area...' We also get emails from different parts of the UK, from people in Birmingham, Scotland, or whatever, asking if we can help, and we're just volunteers, we're a collective, we've never had any paid staff. It's just heart-wrenching. All we can do is signpost them to other organisations who might be able to help.

'Layers of goodwill'

I could talk about LISG for ages. There's all those links we've built up over the last twelve or thirteen years. Like L Fest, the lesbian music and arts festival, emailing us out of the blue, 'Would you like twenty-three tickets?' They actually did that the year before last, but it was too short notice.

'That's great, but have you any idea how much organisation it's going to take?'

So this year, they absolutely got it. They offered us free tickets and they arranged glamping tents, they arranged wellies, torches, someone looked into the cheapest train fares – they got it, which was wonderful. Members could go away for three days and just have a bloody good time. They can enjoy that sense of togetherness and, 'This is where we can be who we are!'

But it's also evidence for their cases. They're forced by the Home Office to have 'evidence', so they've got to document things: lots of happy photographs at events, while having time off from all the stress of the asylum process.

Then we have links with groups like the feminist organisation FiLiA. Two years ago, their conference was in Manchester. It was in October, but I think it was back in about May of that year that they contacted lots of women's organisations in the area and we met in Nexus cafe, around that big table. From that, some of the LISG members spoke at a couple of workshops at FiLiA, and since then the contacts have grown. They gave us some funding for travel and accommodation for their conference last year in Bradford, so about fifteen of us went over there. They've helped us with support letters for various members, as well. It's all about getting those fantastic links.

I love seeing the way that women's confidence grows as they get more involved in LISG. At the first meeting, it's usually, 'Ooh, I don't know what to expect!' and then it's just, 'Oh, I feel relaxed and comfortable.' And you can see the connections between women, particularly if they're from the same country and they share a language; and that sense that they are part of LISG.

The links with the Todmorden and Calderdale women have been fantastic as well. They used to do fundraisers twice a year for various different women's organisations. Once they'd decided that we were going to be the group they give the money to, they let us know and quite a few of us went along. At that time we were working on Grace's claim and Tod has groups of women in their fifties, sixties, seventies. I'll never forget Grace walking into that event. She had no idea of the demographic in Tod. I watched her face. I was thinking, 'I need to see her reaction!' LISG is almost all much younger women – and watching her face as she clocked all these older lesbians, it was a joy to see! But also, I was thinking, 'I needed to see that, because that's going in the letter.'

After that, I was thinking, we need to build her case, so I got in touch with Sorrel – she and her partner were part of that organising group. I said, 'The Home Office don't believe she's a lesbian, because they think all lesbians are young. Would you be able to write anything about your experiences?' So Sorrel and her partner invited me and Grace over to lunch and then Sorrel wrote a letter. Then she said, 'I want to be involved in LISG!'

Since that time, they still do two fundraisers a year at Todmorden, but every single time now, it's for LISG. Before, it was a different group every time, but it's never been any group other than LISG in the last four years. Sometimes, when women have been between accommodation or had to wait for Home Office accommodation, had nowhere to go and been sofa-surfing... Sometimes the Tod women have put women up for a couple of weeks, or offered their home over Christmas – because that can be a really difficult time. And the women who put on the Hebden Bridge Film Festival gave LISG free tickets last year. They're such brilliant links.

So it feels like LISG is growing, and it's not just this one group, it's got those outer layers of all this goodwill, which is fantastic.

I remember someone saying, 'You can see the love in this group,' and other women have said, 'In other groups we get what we're given, but in LISG we have a voice.' There's that sense of ownership: LISG is everyone. That sense of ownership is so important. LISG gives me so much joy and it's about trying to spread that as well. When I gave up my job to become a student, I thought I'd have all this spare time... You can imagine where that's gone!

HOW LISG WORKS

All the women in this book, whether members or volunteers, talk about the impact LISG has made on their lives. But what exactly does LISG do? Here, some of the contributors describe in more detail how the group supports its members.

Listening

Karen M: When a woman made contact, by email or by phone, we would always meet her, with both a volunteer and a member from the group. We'd explain again what LISG was, who we were, and that it's about sexuality. We have to understand that the women have had to live hidden, and then suddenly they're supposed to come here and tell all about it! So we would talk about the fact that there were famous figures in this country who'd still not come out, and that some of us had not. So that discussion is had, and we establish the outline of their case. Now, sometimes you can't stop somebody talking because they need to get it out; and sometimes they're very reticent. At that stage we need to know basic things like, have they got housing support? Are they getting any other support? Have they got any money? Where are they living? Are they safe? Do they need any medical treatment or are they getting it? All that sort of stuff. And if women haven't claimed asylum, we try to persuade them not to claim until we've done that.

Karen S: We start to get a bit of a sense of who they are. We don't push anyone to give any more details than they feel comfortable with – we're not the Home Office! If it's clear that she's not lesbian or bisexual, she's not invited to the group meeting; we point her towards other organisations that can help. That has happened on a couple of occasions. And it's really important for us to be able to say that, truthfully, because the Home Office might say, 'Well, you just accept everyone! You'll write a support letter for anyone!' No. There's a process.

Karen M: We've found over the years that if we get their life story and that forms the basis of their statement, it gets them thinking and helps their solicitor, too. Often, they come to us when they've already been refused, and that creates a lot of work, because once they've been disbelieved – it'll be disbelief, nearly always – it's an uphill struggle against that. The people at the Greater Manchester Immigration Aid Unit are very complimentary about us and the work we do. They simply couldn't put in the hours. I can think of one woman in particular, where we had three meetings of three or four hours each, to get everything down. And sometimes, of course, they're very distressed.

We ask if they have already got legal representation. It's usually a matter of trying to get them into the Immigration Aid Unit; or finding out about their solicitor, if they do have one. Because there are some solicitors out there who don't know what they're doing, don't *care* what they're doing. It's criminal, they should not be taking the money.

Karen S: We get to know her and encourage her to get involved, and we won't write a support letter unless someone has been to at least three of the monthly group meetings. It's like, 'We have to get a sense of who you are, that we're happy to stand up in court and say, "I'm confident that this woman is lesbian or bisexual."'

Writing letters

Karen M: We write letters of support after about three months, if needed, from LISG, but also maybe from individuals within LISG, and we go to court to witness, if possible. And we carry on supporting. LISG has never, to our knowledge, supported anyone who has then been deported. There are some people we've lost contact with, but we always worked on the basis that they would get back in touch with LISG if they were in trouble.

Karen S: It might be that someone's been to three meetings and asked for a support letter, but none of the volunteers feel we know her well enough yet. But however long they've been in LISG, we'll meet with them again one-to-one and go through their case in detail, spending usually at least an hour and a half. If they've had a refusal, we'll go through their refusal documents, looking at why the Home Office didn't believe them and getting the woman's take on it. We might say, 'When they said you acted in this way, what's your view on that?' and she might come out with something that absolutely makes sense, but of course the Home Office has taken it in a completely different context because they don't understand the situation.

Or it might be that they haven't been to court, that they're going for their substantive interview. We'll go through their case right from childhood, everything that's happened, and invariably there's tears – just real, raw emotion there. As well as what's happened and why they had to flee, we'll talk about 'When was the first time you felt different?' And someone could be in floods of tears telling her story, but then she'll think of her first girlfriend, and there's that moment of joy on her face. It's those little unguarded moments: they all go in the letter, those little moments when you can say, '*This* is why I believe her!'

It doesn't feel comfortable that I'm passing judgement. But for the woman who needs to jump through Home Office hoops, I will jump through them with her, at the same time working for a world where those hoops don't exist.

I've actually been asked in court, 'Have you ever refused to write a letter?' and I've been able to say, 'Yes.' It's about keeping the integrity of the LISG letters, so that they carry weight. There's a real 'culture of disbelief' in the Home Office. Their starting point is, 'You're lying.' So it's about giving evidence, to be able to say, 'As a lesbian, this is why I believe *this* woman is a lesbian.'

I think generally the courts do now put weight on our letters. Last year about ten women from LISG got through: some because their court cases were successful, and some because they were successful early on and didn't need to go to court.

Going to court

Sorrel: I think the court cases have been some of the most distressing and emotional times for both members and volunteers. Sometimes there is upset and anger when we know the judge does not believe the woman or her witnesses; sometimes numbness when the Home Office is vindictive; sometimes hope when the judge has listened attentively and with compassion, and sometimes amazement when – very rarely – the judge tells the woman she has her stay. But for most, there is the wait. This is gruelling. Waiting, waiting. Some members have been waiting for years to hear about their claim; some are refused and have to start over again appealing against the decision. As an organisation, the members and volunteers never give up. We have successfully fought for every woman and, so far, no one has been deported.

It has been close. In my first months with LISG, a woman was about to be put on a plane; she was actually at the airport. The volunteers went into action, setting up an appeal, contacting MPs and other high-profile people. She was detained in Yarl's Wood, but the strength of her campaign meant she was released quite quickly. A few months later, she and her partner, both claiming asylum as a couple, were given their leave to remain. I couldn't believe that one minute someone can be about to be deported and the next they have their stay. It reflected the grossly arbitrary nature of the asylum process and the hostile environment in which the women have to cope. I don't know how they do it. It is soul-destroying.

But then there is the other side of LISG women. I remember one fundraising event in Todmorden. The organisers were getting ready, when a group of LISG women burst into the hall, bringing this amazing energy. 'Here we are, we've come to the party!' The whole room came alive. This extraordinary strength of spirit always amazes me and, in that moment, they showed all their potential and love of life. I treasure shared moments with individual LISG members, where we laugh and cry and talk about what's going on. These moments make the mental and emotional trauma that is so palpable less overwhelming. It's sharing at such a deep level and knowing that, 'Yes, here we are,' and 'We will get through this together.'

Afterwards

Karen M: One of the things that happens when the status finally arrives is that all your energy's gone into telling your story and making your life safe; then you are safe but have to face that you're never going home, you're probably never going to see your mum again... We've had several women whose mums have died, and how difficult that is! I think it makes the grieving process much more difficult.

There have also been women in LISG who, for example, have come here to study, then come out while they're here and realise they can't go home. So the trauma they have is not being able to go home, and the phone call, and the reaction from the family. They might not necessarily have been raped or sent to prison, but it doesn't mean they're not traumatised. In a report from Women for Refugee Women, there was a quote where this woman said, 'It's not what happened to me at home that broke my mind, it's what happened to me here!'

You've got women whose struggle has gone on for years and years, who have had to cope with that disbelief, after they've been brave enough to tell. For anybody who has had to emigrate away from their family, when family members start dying, it's so hard. So, they're facing the fact that they're never going to see their siblings, or their friends, or their lovers, again; sometimes they don't know what's happened to their lovers. And, although by the time they get there, a lot of women are already receiving help from mental health services, a lot of them have some sort of struggle or crisis at that point. One woman said to me, 'I don't think I'm repairable. I know I've been here a long time now but I'm not really repairable.' She seems to function, seems to have a life, but every so often she has a crisis.

The volunteers

Karen S: I always think LISG is a really difficult group to come into as a volunteer, because we're all firefighting. We try and mentor new volunteers, but sometimes it's chaos, doing this and doing that, juggling so many different things. So we try and ease women in, but no one's going to give you specific jobs to do. It's like, 'We're a collective, you've got to roll your sleeves up and get stuck in!'

Karen M: We try and work to get women in the group to take on things like the social stuff; it varies from year to year, depending on who's active. But once women get their status, they've got to get their lives sorted out: they've got to find somewhere to live, find a job. They're often working shifts in the care sector, they're often also studying, and there's a natural thing amongst refugees and asylum seekers in general, of wanting to get away from the stigma and not be associated with all that. So some of them leave Manchester. Some do stay in touch, but not that many, really. I remember a woman who came to LISG when she was needing support and stayed on. She was absolutely committed to the group and described it as her family. We hoped there'd be more people like her. There was a real issue that, every time there was a drive for new volunteers, we got a lot of new white volunteers and very rarely attracted black people. I've talked about it on and off, and tried to do something, but I don't think I ever did enough. It rankled with me more and more, that really, we needed to dedicate somebody's energy to getting that balance changed.

Prossy: I love the Karens and everyone, but it was a white group of volunteers. That's not to take anything away from it, but it helped the members to see someone of a different shade as a volunteer, someone the women could talk to and see that it gets better and it can happen. Because it can feel like, 'Will this ever end? Does this *ever* end?' So it's important to hear from someone that it actually does. It does end, you will get there, but it's not a pretty battle, you're not going to get out of it without any scars. You will get scars, you'll be discouraged, you're going to be disbelieved. With some of the first people you talk to, you are going to be saying, 'Hi, I'm a lesbian woman,' and they're going to be saying, 'You're a liar.'

Karen S: We've had women who've been members of LISG and then become volunteers when they got their stay, and that is the ideal. Chipo's in that situation, and there are a couple more women recently. Prossy was a volunteer for a long time and she's been great. But when women get their stay, there's so many other things to do: they need to find accommodation, sign on, think what they're going to do with the rest of their lives. After that euphoria, there's usually a crash, and they've got to pick themselves up. It's great when they do, and when they come back as volunteers. Because, obviously, LISG absolutely should be led by women like that – women who have gone through the asylum process and know how it is – and we should be in

211

the supporting role. That's always been the hope. In the last year or so, we've probably got a more diverse volunteer group than we've ever had in our history, which is great.

'A model that works'

Karen S: Four or five years ago, LISG put on a conference, to try and encourage other groups to be set up as specifically lesbian and bisexual women's asylum groups. I laugh when I think of those organising meetings for the conference, they were just like organised chaos! But it was a really good conference. It was really successful, it was really grass-roots, down to earth; I've got very fond memories. I can't remember how many people came, but the vast majority were women. On the back of that conference, there were two new groups set up: one in Nottingham and one in Liverpool. At some point after that, the one in Liverpool became LGBT rather than just for women. So, we were back to being more or less the only lesbian and bisexual women's asylum group, which was such a shame, because there's such a need out there.

Karen M: Some of the women in LISG will happily go into mixed things; some will go into mixed things but not so happily; but you'll find a lot of the women talking about LISG being the only safe space where they can be who they are. There are so many issues around feeling safe around men, given what might have happened to them.

Karen S: At our last meeting, one of the new volunteers was saying that we need to get information about LISG out there, and I remember the phrase she used: 'LISG has a model that works!' I really liked that. It was what the conference was about – wanting to share that. There's this huge need, and we know this model works: giving evidence and building women's cases; being there in court so a woman's not by herself. So it was a shame it didn't mushroom out from the conference. I hope this book will be another way of getting all that out there, and saying: 'This is who we are; this is how we started. You don't have to know anything about asylum to start with. It's just that fire-in-the-belly stuff – having that passion, seeing that injustice and wanting to do something about it.' And emotionally, physically, it's hard work at times!

'Something that I hope continues'

Prossy: When you travel to a different place, it's difficult to adjust and to find your bearings; but then, imagine that you've also been through trauma, and you've been through things that you wouldn't even know how to start to explain to someone. And some of it is just so unbelievable, even to yourself, that you think, 'If I can't believe that this has happened, how is someone else going to believe me?' It's such a traumatic thing that even you are in denial. So when you arrive here, and you have all those things going on, it's hard to comprehend, and to find a place to go, to find any sort of joy at all.

Then you find places like LISG, and it's a sanctuary that you cannot even put into words. It's not just a support group, it really isn't. It's a support group of sorts, in that they can help you go through your statement and so on; but, in a world where you've been disowned most times by most of the people that you're close to, you go to this place and it's like a hug, not to your body, but to your soul. You start getting back your soul. Because of the way that the sexuality cases are treated, and the sort of evidence that you're supposed to present, you don't know where to start. Places like LISG, where they can help you understand what you're supposed to do, are like gold.

When I arrived, there wasn't any place for refugees or asylum seekers, for a long time. There was nothing specific for LGBT asylum seekers. Then these women started this crazy thing, saying, 'Oh, yeah – we could do something for lesbian and bi women!' I don't even know if they were aware of the chain they started, and I don't think they're even aware to this day of the impact that this sort of support had on people like me. Just to have them there on the street, holding your hand... I thought, 'My own father has just thrown me out like I was yesterday's dinner, and you, the person I've just met – in this strange country where some of the words are over my head and I don't understand the accent, so that I feel like I don't speak English – you're standing here in the rain with me, holding a pen and getting signatures! Either you're crazy, or you're the most amazing person I've ever met in my life!'

They are such incredible women. Look at the things they do for people – not financial, although that helps – but the support and the sisterhood, and being there for you and looking you in the eye, like, 'It's going to work out. We're going to try everything we can.' For many of these women, it's the first time in a long time that they've had someone in their corner, genuinely on their side. And it is the most amazing thing. They are really, really good. Awesome. They've started something that I hope continues, and goes to different places, because there are people out there who don't have this, and it is such a massive gap. I do hope it happens.

~

SUPPORT GROUPS

This is a list of the main organisations mentioned in this book, along with other UK groups that welcome lesbians and asylum seekers.

MANCHESTER

Lesbian Immigration Support Group
The group behind this book! Provides support for lesbian and bisexual women seeking asylum. You can contact LISG or make a donation via their website:
https://lesbianimmigrationsupportgroup.blogspot.com/

First Wednesday
Support and social group for LGBTQ+ people who are in the asylum process.
https://firstwednesday.lgbt/

Greater Manchester Immigration Aid Unit
Exists to advise, support, represent and campaign with people subject to immigration control.
https://gmiau.org/

Metropolitan Church
A welcoming church in South Manchester.
https://metropolitanchurch.org.uk/

Women Asylum Seekers Together
Support group for women of all ages, nationalities, ethnicities, sexual orientation and disabilities who are seeking asylum. Weekly drop-in sessions.
https://www.wastmanchester.com/

OTHER CITIES

BIRMINGHAM

Journey Asylum Seekers Group
Social group, meeting at Birmingham LGBT Centre. Venue also hosts advice surgeries and a range of other groups.
https://blgbt.org/asylum-seekers/

CARDIFF

Glitter Cymru
Social and support group for LGBTQ+ ethnic minority people, including refugees and asylum seekers.
http://glittercymru.org.uk/

GLASGOW

LGBT Unity
Advice and support group for LGBTQ+ asylum seekers.
https://unityinthecommunityglasgow.wordpress.com/unity-lgbt-support-group/

LEICESTER

Free to Fly
Social and support group for LGBTQ+ refugees and asylum seekers. Meetings twice a month.
https://leicesterlgbtcentre.org

LIVERPOOL

Many Hands One Heart
Support network for LGBTQ+ people living in Merseyside who are seeking asylum or are refugees.
https://sahir.org.uk/lgbt/

LONDON

Freedom from Fear to Love
Offers socialising and support for people seeking asylum.
Part of Outcome, the LGBTQ+ service at Islington Mind.
https://www.islingtonmind.org.uk/our-services/outcome/
freedom-from-fear-to-love/

Rainbows Across Borders
Self-help group in Croydon for LGBTQ+ asylum seekers.
https://www.rainbowsacrossborders.org.uk/

NOTTINGHAM

Kairos: Nottingham Lesbian Immigration Support Group
Group of lesbian and bi women including asylum seekers,
refugees and supporters. Offering help through the asylum
application process.
https://www.facebook.com/Kairos-1898790527043600/

SHEFFIELD

Lesbian Asylum Support Sheffield (LASS)
Supporting and empowering LBTQ+ and non-binary
asylum seekers and refugees in Sheffield and across South
Yorkshire. Monthly meeting at Together Women.
https://lassheffield.org.uk/

NATIONAL

African Rainbow Family
Supports LGBTQ+ people of African heritage and wider
BAME groups, including refugees. Based in Manchester
with branches in Leeds, Birmingham and London.
https://africanrainbowfamily.org

British Red Cross
Free emergency support for refugees and asylum seekers.
May include food, clothing and advice.
https://www.redcross.org.uk/get-help/get-help-as-a-refugee

FiLiA
Part of the Women's Liberation Movement. The focus of
their work is an annual women's rights conference.
https://filia.org.uk/

L Fest
National music and arts festival aimed mainly at lesbian
and bi women.
https://lfest.co.uk/

Lesbians and Gays Support the Migrants
Queer activist group standing in solidarity with migrants
and refugees. Groups in London, Brighton and Bristol.
https://www.lgsmigrants.com/

Micro Rainbow
Provides housing, social inclusion and employability
activities to LGBTQ+ asylum seekers and refugees.
https://www.microrainbow.org/

UK Lesbian & Gay Immigration Group
Promotes equality and dignity for LGBTQ+ people who seek
asylum or wish to settle in the UK to be with their partners.
https://uklgig.org.uk/

Women for Refugee Women
Supporting and empowering refugee women.
https://www.refugeewomen.co.uk/

ACKNOWLEDGEMENTS

My personal thanks to all the members and volunteers at LISG, for welcoming me into the group and for all they have taught me. This book could not have been written without the courage and co-operation of the wonderful women whose lives feature in it. It has been a privilege to work with them.

Thanks also to the LGBT Foundation in Manchester, who gave us free space to record the interviews; to Rose Bunker and Kerry Mitchell for typing; and to Helen Sandler at Tollington Press – good friend and most patient editor – for believing in our book and making it a reality.

JT

ABOUT THE EDITOR

Jane Traies is the editor of *Now You See Me: Lesbian life stories* (Tollington, 2018), and author of *The Lives of Older Lesbians: Sexuality, identity and the life course* (Palgrave Macmillan, 2016) and other publications in the field of ageing and sexuality.

As Jay Taverner, she is also joint author with Jacky Bratton of the lesbian historical novels, *Rebellion* (Onlywomen, 1997), *Hearts and Minds* (Diva, 2001) and *Something Wicked* (Onlywomen, 2002). The fourth book in the series is due soon from Tollington.

ALSO FROM TOLLINGTON

Rights of Passage
A play by Clare Summerskill

The script of the groundbreaking drama that brought LGBT asylum stories to the stage

Who is welcome, who is locked up and who is deported?

Using real-life stories, this play explores the struggles and triumphs of LGBT people who have fled to the UK from persecution in anti-gay countries, including Uganda, Iran and Malaysia. Moving, disturbing, but ultimately offering hope through solidarity, *Rights of Passage* is verbatim theatre at its finest.

'The most powerful and accurate portrayal of LGBT asylum seeker stories I've ever watched.'
UK Lesbian and Gay Immigration Group member

Order from your local bookshop or direct by email:
admin@claresummerskill.co.uk
www.claresummerskill.co.uk

Liberty!
A new novel by Jay Taverner

**The long-awaited fourth book in the series
that began with *Rebellion***

Set in the 1780s, *Liberty!* follows gender rebel
Rebecca Wiston on a whirlwind journey of discovery from
New England to revolutionary France, where romance
awaits her in the person of the beautiful aristocrat Annette.

Fleeing from mob violence in Bordeaux, the lovers
face new trials in London before the story shifts to the
Shropshire hills and takes us once again to Brynsquilver,
the lodestone of this series of historical adventures.
There, a mystery is solved and another link forged
in Taverner's unfolding tale of women's love and
resourcefulness across the centuries.

Coming in 2021!